GEOFFREY CHAUCER

Geoffrey Chaucer

LECTURES DELIVERED IN 1932
ON THE WILLIAM J. COOPER FOUNDATION
IN SWARTHMORE COLLEGE

By

JOHN LIVINGSTON LOWES

OXFORD
AT THE CLARENDON PRESS

Oxford University Press, Ely House, London W.1

GLASGOW NEW YORK TORONTO MELBOURNE WELLINGTON
CAPE TOWN SALISBURY IBADAN NAIROBI LUSAKA ADDIS ABABA
BOMBAY CALCUTTA MADRAS KARACHI LAHORE DACCA
KUALA LUMPUR SINGAPORE HONG KONG TOKYO

FIRST EDITION 1934
REPRINTED LITHOGRAPHICALLY IN GREAT BRITAIN
AT THE UNIVERSITY PRESS, OXFORD
1944, 1949, 1956, 1961, 1964, 1969

TO

GEORGE LYMAN KITTREDGE

'Myn owene mayster dere'

PREFACE

THE six chapters which follow were delivered as lectures at Swarthmore College on the William J. Cooper Foundation in January and February 1932, and are published in accordance with the terms of the Foundation. They are printed essentially as they were delivered, except that the second lecture has been split into two chapters, the present second and third. There are undoubtedly those—I should be, I am sure, of the number myself—who will be disturbed by the absence of means by which statements may be controlled and citations verified. But the requirement that the lectures be published as lectures precludes references and notes. Any study such as this, however, must build upon foundations laid by the long line of students and lovers of Chaucer, living and dead. And to them, even though it may be in general terms alone, I record my homage and gratitude.

To Swarthmore College too—'[our] frendschipe nas nat newe to biginne'—the generous response and warmhearted welcome which lectures and lecturer alike received have placed me under a happy debt which may be only acknowledged, never paid.

J. L. L.

29 January, 1933

CONTENTS

I. BACKGROUNDS AND HORIZONS

NOTHING more unlucky, I sometimes think, could have befallen Chaucer than that he should have been christened 'the father of English poetry'. For 'father' in such a context conveys to most of us, I fear, a faint suggestion of *vicarious* glory—the derivative celebrity of parents, otherwise obscure, who shine, moon-like, in the reflected lustre of their sons. What else than progenitors were the fathers of Plato, or Caesar, or Shakespeare, or Napoleon? And so to call Chaucer the father of English poetry is often tantamount to dismissing him, not unkindly, as the estimable but archaic ancestor of a brilliant line. But Chaucer—if I may risk the paradox—is himself the very thing that he begat. He *is* English poetry incarnate, and only two, perhaps, of all his sons outshine his fame. It is with Chaucer himself, then, and not save incidentally with his ancestral eminence that we shall be concerned.

But five hundred and thirty-three years have passed since Chaucer died. And to overleap five centuries is to find ourselves in another world—a *mundus alter et idem*, at once familiar and strange. Its determining concepts are implicit in all that Chaucer, who was of it, thought and wrote. And, woven as they are into his web, they at once lend to it and gain from it fresh significance. To us they are obsolete; in the *Canterbury Tales*, and the *Troilus*, and the *House of Fame* they are current and alive. And it is in their habit as

they lived, and not as mere curious lore, that I mean
to deal with them.

I

Let me begin with the very tongue which Chaucer
spoke—a speech at once our own and yet not ours.
'You know', he wrote, recalling in perfect keeping
Horace by way of Dante—and for the moment I rudely
modernize lines as liquid in their rhythm as smooth-
sliding Mincius—'you know that within a thousand
years is change in form of speech, and words which
were then deemed apt and choice now seem to us wondrous quaint and strange; and yet they spoke them so,
and sped as well in love thereby as men now do'. And
to us, after only half a thousand years, those very lines
are an embodiment of what they state:

> Ye knowe eek, that in forme of speche is chaunge
> With-inne a thousand yeer, and wordes tho
> That hadden prys, now wonder nyce and straunge
> Us thinketh hem; and yet they spake hem so,
> And spedde as wel in love as men now do.

Chaucer himself in his own day saw the change in
English speech progressing, and with characteristic
acumen recognized its menace to the future understanding of his verse. 'And for ther is', he wrote at the
close of the *Troilus*, addressing his 'litel book'—

> And for ther is so greet diversitee
> In English and in wryting of our tonge,
> So preye I god that noon miswryte thee,
> Ne thee mismetre for defaute of tonge.
> And red wher-so thou be, or elles songe,
> *That thou be understonde I god beseche!*

That petition has not gone unheard, yet the obstacle to instant understanding does exist, and I have no intention of belittling it. But I should like to say with emphasis—and I am speaking not to the student of Chaucer but to the lover of books—that it seems more formidable than it is. A bare fraction of the time which we spend in learning to read Homer or Virgil or Dante or Molière or Goethe will enable any of us to read Chaucer as he is meant to be read, to wit, with delight—as Dryden read him, knowing less than we, though seeing more. For it is in words and idioms whose nearness to ours is greater far than their distance is remote that Chaucer's men and women speak— speak, at their best, with a raciness and point and flavour that have never been surpassed. Nor is it a *sine qua non*—and I think I know—to master all the complexities of Middle English in order to follow with intelligence Chaucer's language, and to feel his 'divine liquidness of diction', and the 'divine fluidity' of his verse. It is, I suspect, the awe-inspiring *chevaux de frise* of Chaucerian scholarship which has often scared the laymen for whom Chaucer wrote from entrance upon their rights. That technical erudition, however, may safely be left by the lover of poetry until its results have fertilized the common soil.

But it is not only Chaucer's speech which has undergone transformation. The change in his world is greater still. And the situation which confronts us, to put it in a word, is this. In Chaucer's greatest work we have to do with *timeless creations* upon a *time-deter-mined stage*. And it is one of the inescapable ironies of time that creations of the imagination which are at once of no time and for all time must nevertheless think and speak and act in terms and in ways which are as transient as they themselves are permanent. Their world—the stage on which they play their parts, and in terms of which they think—has become within a few lifetimes strange and obsolete, and must be deciphered before it can be read. For the immortal puts on mortality when great conceptions are clothed in the only garment ever possible—in terms whose import and associations are fixed by the form and pressure of an inexorably passing time. And that is the situation which we have to face.

It is characteristic of Chaucer's penetration that he recognized as a practical problem of his own precisely this complication, and discussed it with singular felicity and point. The story of Troilus and Criseyde which he was retelling was set on the stage of a far-distant time. And the background against which he had to throw his characters and his action was remote from the familiar knowledge of his audience. And in the Proem to his Second Book he faces the difficulty in a passage as charming as it is acute. You know, he says (for it is with the stanza which I have already quoted that he begins), you know how *speech* has changed within a thousand years; yet words now strange were potent enough then. And as it is with words so is it also with the affairs of love:

> . . . in sondry ages,
> In sondry londes, sondry been usages.

And then, in lines compact of exquisite insight and

humour, he warns his hearers—for he was reading the poem aloud—against the risk of allowing changes in manners and customs to confuse their perception of that fundamental human nature common to lovers, alike in London and Troy.

Chaucer's shrewd caveat is no less pertinent now than then. Criseyde and Pandare and the Wife of Bath and Harry Bailly and the Miller and the Reeve and the Squire are more vividly alive to-day than you and I. They are of one blood with Falstaff and Sancho Panza and Tom Jones and Mr. Pickwick and Becky Sharp and Mrs. Proudie and Captain Ahab. But they think in terms and act in ways which are no longer ours, and the stage on which they move is strange to us. And what I wish first of all to attempt is to reconstruct at least a portion of that time-determined stage —to reanimate, in a word, if may be, a few of the notions now obsolete which permeated the thinking of their period.

By Chaucer's world, then, I mean for the moment that complex of conceptions in terms of which he and his contemporaries thought, as we, for example, think (when we think!) in terms of evolution, and electrons, and time-space continuums, and the second law of thermo-dynamics, and an expanding or contracting universe—all of which concepts, in their turn, will give place to other conditioning ideas. But for Chaucer's planes of reference we must go back to a pre-Copernican, pre-Newtonian, pre-Einsteinian world —a world to us fantastic, but less fantastic, perhaps, than ours will be five hundred years from now. For,

once more, as Chaucer wrote to his old friend Scogan
—and the belief lies deep in his philosophy,

> . . . al shal passe that men prose or ryme;
> Take every man his turn, as for his tyme.

And that now remote world of his, with its backgrounds and presuppositions, we must get clear about
for a very definite reason.

For it is not as if Chaucer at one time thought the
thoughts of his period, and at another stopped his
thinking and gave his emotions and his imagination
rein. He was, on the contrary, singularly of a piece.
His poetry did not occupy one compartment of his
brain and his knowledge and his ponderings another.
The two coalesced. All of Chaucer was apt to be
present when he wrote, and the conceptions held in
solution in his thinking were continually precipitated
in his verse. Sometimes they emerged in detail, but
more often, especially when he was writing at high
tension, in swift, passing, and enriching references—
the 'spontaneous overflow' of what he knew. And
even apart from the light they throw on what he
wrote, the modest effort demanded in thinking his
thoughts after him has, like even temporary residence
in a country akin to yet different from our own, the
virtue of enlarging our scope. And every conception
which will concern us survives, in one form or another,
in your speech and mine to-day.

II

It is with backgrounds and bounds alone, then,
that I mean this time to deal, and the background

of backgrounds is Chaucer's universe. How did he think of it? And in what relation does it stand to ours? Let us start, at least, from common ground.

We live in terms of *time*. And so pervasive is that element of our consciousness that we have to stand, as it were, outside it for a moment to realize how completely it controls our lives. For we think and act perpetually, we mortals who look before and after, in relation to hours and days and weeks and months and years. Yesterday and to-morrow, next week, a month from now, a year ago, in twenty minutes—those are the terms in which, wittingly or automatically, we act and plan and think. And to orient ourselves at any moment in that streaming continuum we carry watches on our wrists, and put clocks about our houses and on our public towers, and somewhere in our eye keep calendars, and scan time-tables when we would go abroad. And all this is so utterly familiar that it has ceased to be a matter of conscious thought or inference at all. And—to come to the heart of the business—unless we are mariners or woodsmen or astronomers or simple folk in lonely places, we never any longer reckon with the *sky*. Except for its bearing on the weather or upon our moods, or for contemplation of its depths of blue or fleets of white, or of the nightly splendour of its stars, we are oblivious of its influence. And therein lies the great gulf fixed between Chaucer's century and ours.

For Chaucer and his contemporaries, being likewise human, also lived in terms of time. But their calendar and time-piece was that sky through which

moved immutably along predestined tracks the planets
and the constellations. And no change, perhaps,
wrought by the five centuries between us is more
revealing of material differences than that shift of attitude towards 'this brave o'erhanging firmament', the
sky. And it is that change, first of all, that I wish, if
I can, to make clear.

There could be, I suspect, no sharper contrast than
that between the 'mysterious universe' of modern
science, as interpreters like Eddington and Jeans have
made even laymen dimly perceive it, and the nest of
closed, concentric spheres in terms of which Chaucer
and his coevals thought. The structure of that universe may be stated simply enough. Its intricacies
need not concern us here. About the earth, as the
fixed centre, revolved the spheres of the seven then
known planets, of which the sun and the moon were
two. Beyond these seven planetary spheres lay the
sphere of the fixed stars. Beyond that in turn, and
carrying along with it in its 'diurnal sway' the eight
spheres which lay within it, moved the *primum mobile*,
a ninth sphere with which, to account for certain
planetary eccentricities, the Middle Ages had supple-
mented the Ptolemaic system. We must think, in a
word, of Chaucer's universe as geocentric—the 'litel
erthe', encompassed by 'thilke speres thryes three'.
As an interesting fact which we have learned, we know
it; to conceive it as reality demands an exercise of the
imagination. And only with that mental *volte-face*
accomplished can we realize the cosmos as Chaucer
thought of it.

Now the order of succession of the planetary spheres had far-reaching implications. Starting from the earth, which was their centre, that succession was as follows: Moon, Mercury, Venus, Sun, Mars, Jupiter, Saturn. And implicit in that order were two fundamental consequences—the astrological status of the successive hours of the day, and the sequence of the days of the week. The two phenomena stood in intimate relation, and some apprehension of each is fundamental to an understanding of the framework of conceptions within which Chaucer thought, and in terms of which he often wrote.

There were, then, in the first place—and this is strange to us—two sorts of *hours*, with both of which everybody reckoned. There were the hours from midnight to midnight, which constituted the 'day natural'—the hours, that is, with which we are familiar—and these, in Chaucer's phrase, were 'hours equal', or 'hours of the *clock*'. But there were also the hours which were reckoned from sunrise to sunset (which made up the 'day artificial'), and on from sunset to sunrise again. And these, which will most concern us, were termed 'hours inequal', or 'hours of the *planets*'. And they were the hours of peculiar significance, bound up far more closely with human affairs than the 'hours of the clock'. It is worth, then, a moment's time to get them clear.

They were termed 'inequal' for an obvious reason. For the periods between sunrise and sunset, and sunset and sunrise, respectively, change in length with the annual course of the sun, and the length of their

twelfths, or hours, must of necessity change too.
Between the equinoxes, then, it is clear that the inequal hours will now be longer by day than by night,
now longer by night than by day. And only twice in
the year, at the equinoxes, will the equal hours and the
inequal hours—the hours of the clock and the hours
of the planets—be identical. Moreover, each of the
inequal hours (and this is of the first importance) was
'ruled' by one of the seven planets, and it was as 'hours
of the planets' that the 'hours inequal' touched most
intimately human life. And that brings us at once to
the days of the week, and their now almost forgotten
implications. Why, to be explicit, is to-day Saturday?
And why to-morrow Sunday? To answer those two
questions is to arrive at one of the determining concepts of Chaucer's world.

Let me first arrange the seven planets in their order,
starting (to simplify what follows) with the outermost.
Their succession will then be this:

Saturn, Jupiter, Mars, Sun, Venus, Mercury,
      Moon.

Now Saturn will rule the first hour of the day which,
for that reason, bears his name, and which we still call
Saturday. Of that day Jupiter will rule the second
hour, Mars the third, the Sun the fourth, Venus the
fifth, Mercury the sixth, the Moon the seventh, and
Saturn again, in due order, the eighth. Without
carrying the computation farther around the clock
it is obvious that Saturn will also rule the fifteenth and
the twenty-second hours of the twenty-four which
belong to his day. The twenty-third hour will then

be ruled by Jupiter, the twenty-fourth by Mars, and the twenty-fifth by the Sun. But the twenty-fifth hour of one day is the first hour of the next, and accordingly the day after Saturn's day will be the Sun's day. And so, through starry compulsion, the next day after Saturday *must* be Sunday. In precisely the same fashion—accomplished most quickly by remembering that each planet must rule the twenty-second hour of its own day—the ruling planet of the first hour of each of the succeeding days may readily be found. And their order, so found, including Saturn and the Sun, is this:

Saturn, Sun, Moon, Mars, Mercury, Jupiter, Venus—

then Saturn again, and so on *ad libitum*. And the days of the week will accordingly be the days of the seven planets in that fixed order.

Now Saturn's day, the Sun's day, and the Moon's day are clearly recognizable in their English names of Saturday, Sunday, and Monday. But what of the remaining four—to wit, the days of Mars, Mercury, Jupiter, and Venus, which we call Tuesday, Wednesday, Thursday, and Friday? French has preserved, as also in Lundi, the planetary designations: Mardi (*Martis dies*), Mercredi (*Mercurii dies*), Jeudi (*Jovis dies*), and Vendredi (*Veneris dies*). The shift of the names in English is due to the ousting, in those four instances, of the Roman pantheon by the Germanic. Tiw, Woden, Thor, and Frig (or Freya) have usurped the seats of Mars, Mercury, Jupiter, and Venus, and given their barbarous names to the days. And in

France a fourth, even more significant substitution has taken place. For the sun's day is in French *dimanche*, and *dimanche* is *dominica dies*, the Lord's day. And so between Saturn's planet and Diana's moon is memorialized, along with Mercury and Jupiter and Venus and Mars, the second Person of the Christian Trinity. The ancient world has crumbled, and its detritus has been remoulded into almost unrecognizable shapes. But half the history of Europe and of its early formative ideas is written in the nomenclature of the week. And that nomenclature depends in turn upon the succession of the planetary hours. And it was in terms of those hours that Chaucer and his contemporaries thought.

In the *Knight's Tale*, to be specific, Palamon, Emily, and Arcite go to pray, each for the granting of his own desire, to the temples respectively of Venus, Diana, and Mars. And each goes, as in due observance of ceremonial propriety he must, in the hour of the planet associated with the god to whom he prays. Palamon goes to the temple of Venus, 'And *in hir houre* he walketh forth'. A few lines earlier that hour has been stated in everyday terms: it was 'The Sonday night, er day bigan to springe . . . Although it nere nat day by houres two'—two hours, that is, before sunrise. The day that was springing after Sunday night was Monday, and the hour of Monday's sunrise is the hour of the Moon. And the hour two hours earlier, in which Palamon walked forth, was the hour ruled by Venus, to whose temple he was on the way. And Emily and Arcite, as the tale goes on, performed their pilgrimages at similarly reckoned hours. To Chaucer and his readers all this was familiar matter of the day, as instantly comprehensible as are now to us the hours which we reckon by the clock. For us alas! it has become a theme for cumbrous exposition, because the hours of the planets have vanished, with the gods whose names they bore. All that is left of them is the time-worn and wonted sequence of the seven designations of the days.

Nothing, indeed, is more characteristic of the period in which Chaucer wrote than the strange, twisted mythology, transmogrified and confused, which emerged from the association of the planets and the gods. Not even Ovid had conceived such metamorphoses. For the gods were invested with the attributes of planets, and as such became accountable for the most bizarre occurrences, and kept amazing company. Under the aegis of Mars, to take one instance only, were enrolled the butchers, hangmen, tailors, barbers, cooks, cutlers, carpenters, smiths, physicians, and apothecaries—a band about as 'martial' as Falstaff's Thomas Wart and Francis Feeble. And so, in 'the temple of mighty Mars the rede' in the *Knight's Tale*, there were depicted, together with the 'open werre' which was his by virtue of his godhead, the disastrous chances proceeding from his malign ascendancy as planet—the corpse in the bushes with cut throat, the nail driven, like Jael's, into the temple, the sow eating the child in the cradle, the cook scalded in spite of his long ladle. And from among the members of what Chaucer twice calls Mars' 'divisioun' there were

present—together with the pick-purse, and 'the
smyler with the knyf under the cloke'—the barber and
the butcher and the smith. And in the next paragraph
Mars becomes again 'this god of armes'—god of war
and wicked planet inextricably interfused.

Moreover, as the day and the week were conceived
in terms of planetary sequence, so the year stood in
intricate relation to the *stars*. The sun, with the other
planets, moved annually along the vast starry track
across the sky which then, as now, was called the
zodiac—so called, as Chaucer lucidly explains to 'litel
Lowis' in the *Treatise on the Astrolabe*, because (and
his etymology is sound) '*zodia* in langage of Greek
sowneth [signifies] "bestes" . . . and in the zodiak ben
the twelve signes that han names of bestes'. These
twelve signs, as everybody knows, are Aries, Taurus,
Gemini, Cancer, Leo, Virgo, Libra, Scorpio, Sagit-
tarius, Capricornus, Aquarius, Pisces—or, to follow
Chaucer's praiseworthy example and translate, Ram,
Bull, Twins, Crab, Lion, Virgin, Scales, Scorpion,
Archer, Goat, Water-carrier, Fishes. There they
were, the 'eyrish bestes', as Chaucer calls them in a
delightful passage that will meet us later, and along
their celestial highway passed, from one sign to another, and from house to house, the seven eternal
wanderers. To us who read this—though not to count-
less thousands even yet—the twelve constellations of
the zodiac are accidental groupings, to the eye, of in-
finitely distant suns. To Chaucer's century they were
strangely living potencies, and the earth, in the words
of a greater than Chaucer, was 'this huge stage . . .

whereon the stars in secret influence comment'. Each
sign, with its constellation, had its own individual
efficacy or quality—Aries, 'the colerik hote signe';
Taurus, cold and dry; and so on through the other
ten. Each planet likewise had its own peculiar nature
—Mars, like Aries, hot and dry; Venus hot and moist;
and so on through the other five. And as each planet
passed from sign to sign, through the agency of the
successive constellations its character and influence
underwent change. Chaucer in the *Astrolabe* put the
matter in its simplest terms: 'Whan an hot planete
cometh in-to an hot signe, then encresseth his hete;
and yif a planete be cold, thanne amenuseth [dimi-
nishes] his coldnesse, by-cause of the hote signe.' But
there was far more to it than that. For these complex
planetary changes exercised a determining influence
upon human beings and their affairs. Arcite behind
prison bars cries out:

> Som wikke aspect or disposicioun
> Of Saturne, *by sum constellacioun*,
> Hath yeven us this.

And 'the olde colde Saturnus' names the constellation:

> Myn is the prison in the derke cote . . .
> *Whyl I dwelle in the signe of the Leoun.*

The tragedy of Constance, as the Man of Law conceived it, comes about because Mars, at the crucial
moment, was in his 'derkest hous'. Mars gave, on the
other hand, the Wife of Bath, as she avers, her 'sturdy
hardinesse', because Mars, at her birth, was in the constellation Taurus, which was, in astrological termino-
logy, her own 'ascendent'. And since the constellation

Taurus was also the 'night house' of Venus, certain other propensities which the wife displayed had been thrust upon her, as she cheerfully averred, by the temporary sojourn of Mars in Venus's house, when she was born.

But the march of the signs along the zodiac touched human life in yet another way. 'Everich of thise twelve signes', Chaucer wrote again to his little Lewis, 'hath respecte to a certein parcelle of the body of a man and hath it in governance; as Aries hath thyn heved, and Taurus thy nekke and thy throte, Gemini thyn armholes and thyn armes, and so forth.' And at once one recalls Sir Toby Belch and Sir Andrew Aguecheek in *Twelfth Night*. 'Shall we not set about some revels?' asks Sir Andrew. 'What shall we do else?' replies Sir Toby. 'Were we not born under Taurus?' 'Taurus!' exclaims Sir Andrew, 'that's sides and heart.' 'No, sir,' retorts Sir Toby, 'it is legs and thighs.' And you may still pick up, in the shops of apothecaries here and there, cheaply printed almanacs, designed to advertise quack remedies, in which the naked human figure is displayed with lines drawn from each of the pictured zodiacal signs—Ram, Bull, Crab, Scorpion—to the limbs or organs, legs, thighs, sides, or heart, which that particular sign (in Chaucerian phrase) 'hath in governance'. It is not only in worn stone and faded parchments that strange fragments of the elder world survive.

I spoke a moment ago of our modern devices for telling time. To the pilgrims on the road to Canterbury the sky was not only calendar but clock. When

that astute observer Harry Bailly, who already knew
from the position of the sun that the day was April
eighteenth, further remarked that the shadow of every
tree was of the same length as the body erect that
caused it, and from that perceived that the sun had
climbed forty-five degrees, he thereupon concluded
that for that day, in that latitude, it was ten o'clock.
When Chaucer himself, as the Manciple ended his
tale, observed that the sun had descended so low from
the south line that it was not twenty-nine degrees in
height, he reckoned that it was four of the clock, since,
in addition, his shadow at that time was about eleven
feet in length. When Chaunticlere, his seven wives
walking by his side, cast up his eyes to the bright sun,
that had run its course in the sign of Taurus twenty-
one degrees, he (being a fowl of preternatural astuteness) knew at once that it was nine o'clock, and crew,
and announced to Madame Pertelote that the sun had
climbed up the heaven forty degrees and one. And
Criseyde in the Grecian camp vows to Troilus that
she will return to Troy when the moon, which is just
leaving the Ram, has passed out of the Lion—that is,
she adds (and adds correctly), upon the tenth day.
The sky to Chaucer and his contemporary readers
was still a pictured scroll, whose once familiar symbols
we no longer read.

But the signs of the zodiac and the ceaseless movements of the planets through them touched human
life in still more intimate ways. Here are a few lines,
to take but a single instance, from Chaucer's account
in the Prologue of his Doctour of Phisyk, like whom

—for he was one of Chaucer's nonpareils—there was no other in the world:

For he was grounded in astronomye.
He kepte his pacient a ful greet del
In houres, by his magik naturel.
Wel coude he fortunen the ascendent
Of his images for his pacient.
He knew the cause of everich maladye,
Were it of hoot or cold, or moiste, or drye,
And where engendred, and of what humour;
He was a verrey parfit practisour.

To us it is odd that the first professional qualification of the doctor to be mentioned should be his grounding in *astronomy*. But that is again because to us the hours of the planets no longer exist. To Chaucer's contemporary readers the necessity of a physician's expert knowledge of astronomy was as obvious as to us the indispensability of a surgeon's grounding in anatomy. For the doctor's remedies had to be administered at the proper planetary hours. And those were the hours at which the constitution of the patient and the constitution of a sign or planet were in due correspondence. For human beings, as in a moment we shall see, were compounded of the four elements in definite admixtures—hot and moist, hot and dry, cold and moist, cold and dry. But so were likewise constituted the planets and the zodiacal signs—Mars hot and dry, Venus hot and moist, Taurus cold and dry, and so on. And the eternal movement of seven variously constituted planets through twelve diversely constituted signs was bound at some moment to bring about in the heavens a conjunction of elements which stood in such relation to their maladjusted mixture in the patient as would render the application of the proper remedy effective. And it was expert knowledge of the intricate relations between the elemental characters of planets, signs, and sick man taken together which the medieval doctor had to have. His 'natural magic' was precisely that recondite skill.

But it also included something more. What were the doctor's 'images'? And what did he do to render their ascendant fortunate? As for the term 'ascendant' it is enough to say that both planetary and zodiacal positions are again, though in a different way, involved. But a concrete example of an 'image' will serve as the most illuminating comment which I can make.

Arnaldus of Villanova—or, as Chaucer calls him, 'Arnold of the Newe Toun'—is a figure of capital importance in the development of medieval medicine. And Arnaldus, who lived a century before Chaucer, sets down in one of his treatises the specifications for twelve seals, or 'images', such as he himself is known to have employed in his own practice. And here, translated from Arnold's Latin, is the prescription for the first of the twelve.

Here begin the Seals of Master Arnaldus
In the name of the living Father our Lord Jesus Christ: Take purest gold, and let it be melted as the sun is entering the Ram, that is on the 15th Kalends April [which was the middle of March]. Then let there be modelled of it a round seal, and while it is being moulded into a round you shall say: Rise, light of the world, Jesu true lamb who bearest the sins of the world, and lighten our darkness. And let there be said the Psalm: O Lord, our Lord,

&c. And when it is made, then let it be laid away. [You will remember that in the *Squire's Tale* the artificer of the steed of brass 'knew ful many a *seel*', and '*wayted* many a constellacion'. And so this seal must await the proper constellation, for the account goes on:] And after the Moon enters Cancer or Leo, let there be graven on one side the figure of a ram, while the Sun is in the Ram, and about the circumference Arahel tribus Juda, quinque et septem. And on the other side, about the circumference, let these most sacred words be graven: The word was made flesh and dwelt among us. And in the midst, Alpha and Omega and Sanctus Petrus.

This most precious seal has virtue against all demons and mortal enemies, and against the wiles of the devil, and it is efficacious for gaining wealth and winning favour, and it alleviates dangers and taxes [would that it were still efficacious to-day!], and it is potent against lightning and tempests and floods, and against the violence of winds and the pestilences of the air. And he who carries it shall be honoured and feared on all occasions. And in the house in which it is none shall have power to harm that house or those who dwell in it. And it has virtue against demoniacs and frenetics and maniacs and squinantics, and all diseases of the head and of the eyes, and against ailments in which rheum descends from the head. And in general I may say that it averts all ill and confers all good [patent medicine advertisements have pious parentage!]; and let him who carries it shun so far as he can (inquantum poteris) uncleanness and lechery and other mortal vices, and let it be worn on the head with reverence and honour.

And so the virtue of sun and moon and constellations unites with the potency of Trinity and saints, and the spell of sacred words and occult formulas, against demons and tempests and pestilences, and taxes and colds in the head. And seldom have high and homely been more alluringly conjoined than in those planetary images, the skyey influence of which the Doctour of Phisyk knew how to render fortunate.

I am not sure, indeed, that the most fundamental divergence between Chaucer's century and ours has not been in the shift of attitude that has come about toward the starry heavens and their phenomena. The sky of the planets and constellations was in a sense a *mundus alter et idem*, with which our own was somehow both intimately and inescapably involved. Earth and stars were far closer together then than now, and the planets and the constellations, endowed with human qualities, were baleful or friendly, as the case might be, but never quite alien or aloof. It was a determinate, humanly comprehensible universe. And one looks back with something like nostalgia to its structural neatness and succinctness from the unrepresentable, inconceivable, affrighting universe of contemporary science, or even from the universe of modern poetry,

> Whose farthest hem and selvage may extend
> To where the roars and flashings of the flames
> Or earth-invisible suns swell noisily,
> And onward into ghastly gulfs of sky,
> Where hideous presences churn through the dark—
> Monsters of magnitude without a shape,
> Hanging amid deep wells of nothingness.

Beside that, which past question is the truer picture, Chaucer's cosmography has endearing qualities.

III

And now let us turn, for contrast, from the macrocosm to Chaucer's microcosm, man.

Barring the stock phrase 'flesh and blood', there are few more compact summaries of our conventional lay thinking about the human frame than two lines of a fragment scrawled by Byron on the back of a manuscript of the first Canto of *Don Juan*—a stanza written, as he states with engaging candour three lines later, when he was 'drunk exceedingly':

> I would to Heaven that I were so much clay,
> As I am *blood, bone, marrow*, passion, feeling.

And that loose and divinely simple string of components fairly represents our normal, commonplace conception of those elements which will one day be even more succinctly summarized as 'dust'. We know, to be sure, for science has told us, that we are in fact far more fearfully and wonderfully compounded than that. But however concretely we think of our bodily constituents, we think of them *schematically* not at all. But to think of them as Chaucer and his century conceived them, we must enter once more a world almost as neatly schematized as that of the spheres. And the conceptions embodied in it have permeated speech and literature alike for centuries before and after Chaucer.

There was, in the first place, the basic doctrine, inherited by the Middle Ages from antiquity, of the four elements—earth, water, air, and fire, or, in terms of their qualities, dry, moist, cold, and hot. And only through that conception of the elements can medieval physiology, psychology, and often even characterization be understood. 'Does not our life', asks Sir Toby Belch, as Chaucer might have asked two centuries before him—'does not our life consist of the four elements?' 'Faith,' replies Sir Andrew, 'so they say.' But *how* does our life, so understood, thus consist? Well, out of the conception of the elements grew the doctrine of the *complexions*—that is to say, of certain definite interweavings or combinations of the elements. And with each of these intermixtures was associated a corresponding fluid, or *humour*. To be clear I must again for a moment be specific. The combination of hot and moist produced the sanguine complexion or temperament, of which the corresponding humour was blood. Hot and dry combined gave the choleric complexion or character, the humour of which was choler or bile. Cold and moist in combination gave the phlegmatic; cold and dry the melancholy complexion, with their respective humours phlegm and black bile. And complexion and humour were virtually interchangeable terms, equivalent in each case roughly to one's physical or mental idiosyncrasy or character.

Now let me turn to what, at first blush, is the most unlikely source of information possible—to an account, namely, of the table decorations at the great dinner of a fourteenth-century English franklin. For these 'sotilties' or decorated figures represent the four humours or complexions, and to each is attached a descriptive Latin motto. I shall quote but the first, which sets forth the marks of the *sanguine* complexion:

Largus, amans, hilaris, ridens, rubeique coloris,
Cantans, carnosus, satis audax, atque benignus.

That is to say, the man of sanguine complexion will be free handed, a lover, cheerful, given to laughter, ruddy of face; fond of singing, fleshy, bold, but not too bold, and kind hearted. The list reads like the diagnosis of a palmist, as do the other three which describe, in like detail, the choleric, phlegmatic, and melancholy temperaments. And in each case stress is laid on the detail of colour. As the man of sanguine complexion is ruddy of face, so the choleric man is of saffron hue (*croceique coloris*); the phlegmatic man is pale of face (*facie color albus*); the melancholy man is saffron-yellow (*luteique coloris*). And all four descriptive couplets hail by devious ways from the medieval treatises on medicine.

Now let me read the well-known line about Chaucer's Franklin:

Of his *complexioun* he was *sangwyn*.

To us, who think the thoughts which words stir in us now, the line means simply that the hue of the Franklin's face was florid or ruddy. To Chaucer and his readers it meant that only as an incident. What for them it did essentially, was to place the Franklin forthwith in a familiar category—the category of those free-handed, full-bodied, kind-hearted, cheerful people to which the rest of the description in the Prologue proves him to belong. The line does not describe his looks; it is an epitome of his character. And both 'sanguine' and 'complexion' are terms which you and I freely use to-day in senses still determined by the forgotten categories. For Chaucer's world is the world in which ours has its roots, and it yet survives in words and in usages which have drawn their colour from its conceptions. And the attempt to think its thoughts after it has a value quite beyond the light which it throws on Chaucer. For it enriches our understanding of that amazing continuity which through centuries of sweeping change persists.

Let me turn, now, to a delightful passage in which the erudite medical lore of the complexions is irradiated with Chaucer's humour. And the account of the Doctour of Phisyk will thereby have further light thrown on it too. Dreams have come in these days, thanks chiefly to the potent influence of Freud, to play a curious part in our thinking. But dreams were a subject of interest no less keen in Chaucer's day, and precisely as the Freudian psychology employs them as a means of diagnosis, so fourteenth-century physiology made use of them. And the key to the meaning of dreams as then conceived lay, not in the dreamer's suppressed desires, but in the behaviour of the complexions. In that diverting tale of Madame Pertelote and Chauntecleer, the cock has dreamed one night of a fearsome beast whose colour was 'bitwixe yelwe and red'. And since Chauntecleer, despite his astronomical erudition, is naïvely superstitious, with a simple faith in signs, he is almost dead with fear. But the incomparable Madame Pertelote,

c

the favourite among his seven wives, is a rationalistic and scientifically minded fowl, and she proceeds to analyse his dream. Dreams, she points out, are engendered of *complexions*, when the humours are in too great abundance in a man. If one dreams of *red* things, she explains, it is because the red bile of the choleric complexion is in excess; if one dreams of *black* things, it is because the black bile of the melancholy complexion is too abundant. In the first case, you will dream of arrows, and of fire with red flames, and of great beasts about to bite you; whereas an excess of the melancholy humours makes you cry out in sleep for fear of black bears, or black bulls, or black devils on the point of seizing you. And, she remarks, she could tell all about the other humours too.

Now Madame Pertelote, in the person of Geoffrey Chaucer, had read to good purpose in the great medieval authorities upon medicine. For her method of diagnosis is precisely theirs, and you will find her very examples in them too. And I know no more fascinating reading of its sort than those portions of the works of Arnaldus de Villanova, and the similar treatises of Chaucer's 'Bernard, and Gatesden, and Gilbertyn', which rehearse the things you dream of when this, that, or the other complexion is out of equilibrium. Nor have ever their ponderous pages been turned to such irresistibly humorous account as here— unless it be when, a few lines later, Madame Pertelote prescribes her remedies. But that is another story.[1]

---

[1] It must, I think, be carried a little farther here. For Madame Pertelote includes in her prescription 'digestyves of wormes'. And that has been

There is a no less diverting instance of the pervasiveness of the conceptions we have been discussing in another passage, of a dozen lines, in which the lore of the planets, and the traits of the days of the week, and the idiosyncrasies of lovers, have all rolled their sweetness up into one ball with the complexions. Arcite, in the *Knight's Tale*, much in love, is singing lustily, when suddenly (I am closely paraphrasing Chaucer) he falls into a study, as do those lovers in their curious ways—now in the tree-tops, now down in the briars, now up, now down, like a bucket in a well. *Just as on Friday* (Chaucer goes on), now the sun shines, now the rain falls fast, just so can changeful Venus overcast the hearts of her folk. Just as her day is changeful, just so she changes the way in which she acts. *Seldom is Friday like the rest of the week.*

regarded, with solemn unanimity, as Chaucer's admittedly clever device to make the remedy fit the fowl. But Chaucer was far too consummate an artist to invent when *facts* played into his hand. And the sublimated humour of Madame Pertelote's prescription, with its blended congruity and incongruity, rests on the fact (which Chaucer knew, if we do not) that in the standard treatise *De Medica Materia* of Dioscorides, in the chapter (ii. lix) 'De Vermibvs Terrae', worms are prescribed as a remedy for tertian fevers (*Finiunt iidem [vermes terreni] tertianas febres*). And it is for 'a fevere terciane' that Madame Pertelote prescribes her 'wormes'.

Chauntecleer, it may be added, was happier than his human fellow sufferers. For Dioscorides suggests that the worms be boiled with goose-grease (*cum anserino adipe elixi*), or prepared as a decoction with oil (*cum oleo decocti*), or ground up and drunk with one's food (*triti et cum pasto poti*). And Pliny notes in Book XXX of the *Natural History*, chapter viii, that it is *de rigeur* that one's worms should be drunk with wine (*iubent et vermes terrenos bibi ex vino*). And if all this should seem to be breaking a butterfly—once a worm!—upon the wheel, I can only observe that 'wormes' is a symbol of all the wealth of Chaucer's learning characteristically flowering in a single word.

Why, now, granting the statement, is Friday unlike the other days of the week? It is, briefly, because Venus is hot and moist. In other words, her planet is of the sanguine complexion, and so not only hot and moist but *benevolus et benignissimus* too. If, then, the other days of the week have been wet, Venus on her day, Friday, by virtue of her hotness, benevolently dries the moisture up, and brings clear skies. If, on the other hand, the previous days of the week have been dry, it is her benignant moisture that now comes into play, and brings the needed rain. It is all as simple as 'two and two make four'. And you may find that perspicuous elucidation where I found it— in that thirteenth-century repository of scientific lore, the *De naturis rerum* ('Of the Natures of Things') of Alexander Neckham. 'What nedeth', as Chaucer was wont to say—'What nedeth wordes mo?'

It would take us too far afield to do what I should greatly like to do—to consider, that is, the bearing of the doctrine of the humours upon the malady of *love*, as the Middle Ages and Chaucer with them, conceived it, and to follow it into the racy and erudite pages of Burton's great treatise on 'Love and Love-Melancholy' in the *Anatomy*. And I should like, as I may not, to comment on Hamlet's inclusion, among the 'vicious moles of nature', of 'the o'ergrowth of some complexion'—a phrase which is identical in sense with Madame Pertelote's 'superfluitee' of some one humour. But in order to exemplify once more that stubborn continuity which persists through ceaseless change, I shall quote those lines from the Induction to *Every Man out of his Humour* in which Ben Jonson gives the key to a conception of comedy which in essentials was Dickens's too, and even, at times, George Meredith's. We know—or think we know— what we are, but we should know much better both ourselves and our stock notions if on occasion we pondered our intellectual ancestry and theirs. Here, then, are Ben Jonson's lines:

> . . . in euery humane bodie
> The choller, melancholy, flegme, and bloud,
> By reason that they flow continually
> In some one part, and are not continent,
> Receiue the name of Humors. Now thus farre
> It may by Metaphore applie it selfe
> Vnto the generall disposition,
> As when some one peculiar qualitie
> Doth so possesse a man, that it doth draw
> All his affects, his spirits, and his powers
> In their confluctions all to runne one way,
> This may be truly said to be a Humor.

Every Man in his Humour and *Every Man out of his Humour* still rest, then, both in their titles and in their determining conception, upon the notion of 'the o'er-growth of some complexion'. And when you and I speak of So-and-so as 'good humoured' or 'ill hum-oured', or find ourselves in a 'good humour' or a bad one, we are still, however unwittingly, speaking in terms of that balanced or unbalanced mixture of the four elements which once was thought to constitute us what we are. The concepts of Chaucer's world still mould your speech and mine.

IV

What now, finally, of Chaucer's world in the narrower sense—that fixed and tiny spot which was the centre of the circling spheres? It was, in the first place, we must always remember, thought of constantly in its relation to those nine surrounding spheres. One of the books which most powerfully influenced Chaucer was Boethius *On the Consolation of Philosophy*. And in a striking passage Boethius dwells on the relative minuteness of the earth. It is but 'a prikke' (that is, a pin-point) as compared with the greatness of the heavens, and even of that 'litel regioun of this worlde' only the fourth part is inhabited by living things. And if, as Boethius points out, from that fourth part is withdrawn the space which deserts and marshes and sea take up, the earth inhabited by man is 'the leste prikke of thilke prikke'—the tiniest pin-point of a pin-point. And so, in the *Parlement of Foules*, Scipio is shown, from a starry place, 'the litel erthe, that heer is'—as the ghost of Troilus, also, which had ascended to the concave of the seventh sphere, looks down through the spheres behind him to 'This litel spot of erthe, that with the see Enbraced is'. And that reference to the encircling sea brings us to the earth as conceived without immediate reference to the spheres.

Chaucer's gay little ballade 'To Rosamounde' begins gracefully with a topographical compliment:

> Madame, ye ben of al beaute shryne
> As fer as cercled is the mappemounde.

Now Chaucer's *mappa mundi*—his map of the world

—lay in his mind as a definite shape. And we may picture it vividly enough by turning the pages of Santarem's great *Atlas*, where in scores of medieval *mappamondes* Europe, Asia, and Africa lie folded close together, three cells within the circle of the Ocean stream, like the embryo of the later world. Gower, in that dreadfully long-winded treatise on the education of Alexander, which is apt to drive us panic stricken from its copious detail, speaks of setting

> . . . proprely the bounde
> After the forme of mappemounde,
> Thurgh which the ground be pourparties
> Departed is in thre parties,
> That is Asie, Aufrique, Europe,
> The whiche under the hevene cope,
> Als ferr as streccheth eny ground,
> Begripeth al this Erthe round.

And so in the *Mappamondes* Europe and Africa form the northern and southern quarters respectively of the western half of the habitable world, while the whole of the eastern segment is given up to Asia,

> For that partie was the beste
> And double as moche as othre tuo.

Between Europe and Asia the Tanaïs, the modern Don, forms the boundary line, and

> Fro that into the worldes ende
> Estward, Asie it is algates,
> Til that men come unto the gates
> Of Paradis, and there ho.

And the gates of Paradise, with the castle of Gog and Magog, are there, graphically pictured on the maps. And about the three continents plus Paradise lies

    . . . thilke See which hath no wane,
    [Y-]cleped the gret Occeane.

If, however, you desire to simplify Gower—an always laudable enterprise—draw a circle and bisect it north and south, and then bisect from east to west the western half.

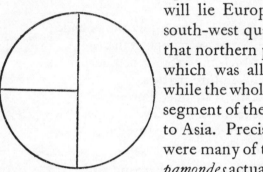

Within the north-west quadrant, roughly speaking, will lie Europe; within the south-west quadrant will lie that northern piece of Africa which was all then known; while the whole of the eastern segment of the circle belongs to Asia. Precisely so, in fact, were many of the oldest *mappamondes* actually drawn, and an early Italian treatise so describes them: 'a T within an O shows the design, through which in three parts was parcelled out the world'. There was as yet no *West*. It was only Dante's Ulysses who, turning the poop of his ship to the morning and its prow to the setting sun, had seen beyond the equator the stars of the other pole.

But east and south and north, no less, were bounded by the unknown. And the *mappamondes* of Chaucer's day—like that in a manuscript of Higden's *Polychronicon*, or the greater one in Hereford Cathedral—were rimmed by startlingly pictured forms of their monstrous and uncanny denizens. I have elsewhere said my say about them, and shall not repeat it here. But from distant regions within those ends of the earth came drifting along the trade-routes and following in the wake of the Crusades, strange rumours and bits of distorted information, which gave scope to fantastic imaginings. North, south, and east had each its peculiar marvels. There is a legend—I wish I could think it something more—that in 1360, the year in which Chaucer was ransomed as prisoner of war, a clerk of Oxford, Nicholas de Linna, passed beyond the Northern Islands and took observations with his astrolabe of those remote boreal regions which he visited. And in the preface to his *Treatise on the Astrolabe* Chaucer promised 'litel Lowis' to give, in the Third Part which was never written, 'many another notable conclusioun' on the authority of one 'frere N. Lenne'. But the identification of the two, which was first made three centuries later, rests on evidence unhappily far too shadowy to trust. Some such voyage, however, may have been made in Chaucer's lifetime, and about it Chaucer may have heard. But it was rather with such marvels as the Magnetic Rock and the fabulous Lebermeer—which lay at the outermost bounds of the northern world, except when it found itself, as it sometimes did, in the Orient —that the unknown north was associated in men's minds.

Strange news filtered, too, from the mysterious depths of equatorial Africa—tales of that brood of captivating monsters whose effigies adorned the southern borders of the early maps, and to hear of some of whom Desdemona seriously inclined. But it was across the east that the wellnigh prehistoric trade-routes lay, mere threads of trodden territory between huge, looming hinterlands of the unknown. And it was that tantalizing and for ever beckoning east which became *par excellence* the land of marvels. And some of its wonders the *Squire's Tale* makes it clear that Chaucer knew.

I suspect there are few ways in which one can acquire more quickly a feeling of that delight in marvels which in the Middle Ages was centred upon the east, than through some acquaintance with the famous *Letter of Prester John*, and through it with that enigmatical figure itself, and his fabulous land of Pentexoire. Texts or versions of the *Epistola* were widely current in Chaucer's day, and he was not the man, if it came his way, to pass it by. At all events, a few 'facts' about Pentexoire will give us at least an inkling of the notions which Chaucer's century harboured about the mysterious east.

In Pentexoire, for one thing, is the Sandy Sea, the *mare arenosum*, which ebbs and flows like the tide. The Fountain of Youth is near it, which varies its taste every hour through the day and night, and in which are the stones *nudiosi*, which the eagles carry off to clear their sight—stones which, when worn on mortal fingers, after weaving of the proper spell, render the wearer invisible. Beyond the Sea lies a river the sands of which are precious stones; and sometimes this River of Gems flows through the Sandy Sea, for it is, indeed, the Sabbatic River, flowing six days and resting the seventh, which keeps the ten tribes of the Children of Israel from crossing into the land of Prester John. And in one part of the desert in which the Sea lies is a people with round feet, like horses' hoofs; and in another part is Chaucer's Land of Femenye itself— 'ane land (to quote a Scottish version of the *Letter*) callit þe vemenland, quhar þair is na man nor na man dar byd our ane yeir . . . and quhen þai pleiss till ride one þair inimeiss, þai ar ane hundreth thousand ridand ladeis witht out þame þat passis one fut . . . And þai ar werray stark and cruell'. And in the Sandy Sea the *monoculi* go a-fishing, and not far away is the Castle of Gog and Magog, and the Land of Melliflôr. I have no idea that Chaucer, who was apt to know chalk from cheese, looked on all this or its like as anything else than stuff for his loom—as the stage, in a word, on which to bring magic mirrors and steeds of brass and rings which give to their wearer understanding of the speech of birds. But the *Squire's Tale* does reveal his wholesome taste for wonders in their proper place, and it is not without interest that the donor of 'the virtuous ring and glass, And the wondrous horse of brass On which the Tartar King did ride' was, in Chaucer's tale, 'the king of Arabie and of Inde'. And by that title Prester John was known.

And since in another connexion we have touched upon medieval science, it is worth a further moment to observe that in Pentexoire were extraordinary anticipations, which seem to have passed unnoticed, of certain modern methods of transferring power. For Prester John—and I am following closely the narratives—has a mill run by wind carried from certain lofty mountains 'twenty milestones to the eastward', through a mighty subway, with which are connected two thousand smaller ones, and this system is duplicated for west, north, and south. And as for *dynamos*, in another mill in Pentexoire is machinery so delicate that in a thousand years the apparatus does not vary by a hair. For the great wheel of this mill is of gold, and in Pentexoire are wise masters who know all the lore of magnets as it is written in the book *Lapidario*. They take, then, as many gold-drawing magnets as are needed, and lay them on the floor above the wheel. And through their inherent energy they draw the wheel towards them powerfully. On the pavement beneath lie similar magnets which draw in the opposite direction. *Die obern ziechent, die undern triben*—the upper pull, the lower push, and so the wheel cannot stand still, but must run back and forth, round and round unceasingly—*hin und her, umb und umb, yemer mer*. And so the mill is run!

The body of Chaucer's 'seint Thomas of Inde' (whether Chaucer knew it or not) is itself, indeed, as another version of the *Epistola* declares, a glorified mill-wheel of a similar sort—except that, through a different distribution of the magnets, St. Thomas remains motionless, *in statu quo*. For his body is cased in iron, and stays in the air, Elysaeus tells us, through the virtue of four precious stones. They are called (and I am quoting) adamant, and are placed one in the pavement, a second in the roof, and one in one angle, another in another, of the sepulchre. The lower mag-

net does not allow the iron coffin to ascend, the upper
to descend, the two in the angles to move hither or
thither. And the Apostle hangs suspended in the
midst—*Apostolus autem est in medio.*

Now these were notions current in Chaucer's day—
planetary hours, and spheres, and seals, and signs of
the zodiac, and elements, and humours, and the lore
of magnets, and Anthropophagi, and astrolabes—
notions which lay in the background of men's minds
then, precisely as now, in your mind and mine, float
relativity, and wireless, and Freud, and planets beyond
the for ever hourless spheres of Uranus and Neptune,
and the convergence, through the air-ways, of the
Antipodes, and Ur of the Chaldees, and the Neander-
thal man. There those were, and here these are—
trivial and momentous, basic and accidental—conditioning and colouring the expression of a period. But
hours and elements and mythological survivals are not
Chaucer. For Chaucer lives, not by virtue of what he
thought about the spheres and the complexions and
the segments of the circle of the earth, but through
the characters which he created and the stories which
he told, and the art which made both characters and
narratives immortal. Yet even so he could not, nor
can you, nor I, put off that muddy vesture of decay
which every period weaves of its own passing thoughts
and theories about enduring things. For the immortal, let me say once more, puts on mortality when, as
it must, it clothes itself in the garment woven of the
transitory speech and concepts of its age. And it is
wise to know that vesture, and to recognize that it

is accidental, lest otherwise it be confounded with the essential which at times it veils. And that is my warrant for spending a preliminary hour upon the obsolete.

II. THE WORLD OF AFFAIRS

THERE is in all of Chaucer's work one passage and one only in which he makes even the slightest reference to the manifold affairs and occupations of his crowded life. The irrepressible Eagle in *The House of Fame* is blithely reproaching him with his ignorance of what is going on not only in far countries but even among his very neighbours at his doors:

> For whan thy labour doon al is,
> And hast y-maad thy rekeninges,
> In stede of reste and newe thinges,
> Thou gost hoom to thy hous anoon;
> And, also domb as any stoon,
> Thou sittest at another boke,
> Til fully daswed is thy loke,
> And livest thus as an hermyte,
> Although thyn abstinence is lyte.

And in that precious glimpse of Chaucer, back at home after the books of the Custom House are closed, reading, reading till his eyes dazzle in his head, are brought together at one stroke the two most powerful influences that made him what he was—his immersion in affairs, and his absorption in his books. Had either been wanting the *Troilus* and the *Canterbury Tales* had never been. We have, in a word, to deal with two worlds, in each of which Chaucer lived —two worlds which stood to each other in sharpest contrast, yet which, through his peculiar genius, merged into one.

Of those dominant influences which went to the making of Chaucer, the first is the vivid and diversified life of the England in which his long official career was spent—the school in which his knowledge of men was gained. And even the barest sketch of that career throws into strong relief the schooling of a poet as paradoxical in seeming as in reality it was divinely right.

Chaucer's earlier years—and this it is essential to remember—were spent in circles which were saturated with French culture. His name first appears, in extant documents, in 1357, when he was between thirteen and seventeen years old. It is in a Household Account Book of Elizabeth, Countess of Ulster, the wife of Lionel, Duke of Clarence, third son of Edward III, some parchment fragments of which survive, lining the covers of a manuscript. And among other items is record of the purchase, for Geoffrey Chaucer, of one paltock from a paltock-maker in London, a pair of red and black (*nigro et rubro*) breeches, and a pair of shoes. And in Elizabeth's service he was (not unlike his own Arcite, who was 'Page of the chambre of Emelye the brighte') with little doubt a page.

The same fragmentary records give us fleeting glimpses of the young Countess—she was only twenty-four, and Lionel nineteen—moving with her retinue, of which Chaucer was a member, through England, between great houses and royal residences in London, Reading, Hatfield, Woodstock, Windsor, and Liverpool; present at splendid court festivities; and even visiting the lions in the Tower of London. Two years later, in 1359, Chaucer, like his own debonair 'yong Squyer', crossed with a formidable army, led by Edward III himself, to invade France; was taken prisoner near Rheims; ransomed with others by the King; and at once sent back across the Channel with dispatches. Then there comes in the records a gap of seven years, from 1360 to 1367. And it seems more than probable, as has recently been keenly argued, that the sixteenth-century tradition that Chaucer was a student at the Inner Temple rests on fact, and that part, at least, of the period for which known records remain silent was spent in legal training for just such diplomatic business and official trusts as those upon which he shortly entered.

At all events, when he next appears he is a member of the household of Edward III, where, for another seven years, until his appointment as Controller of the Customs, he held the rank of yeoman or esquire. And it takes but little imagination to realize, in the light of an extract quoted by Professor Manly from the *Household Book of Edward IV* (which was based upon that of Edward III) the impressions stored from this period:

These Esquires of houschold of old be accustomed, winter and summer, in aftcrnoons and evenings, to draw to Lords' chambers within court, there to keep honest company according to their skill, in talking of chronicles of kings, and of other policies, or in piping, or harping, singing, or martial acts, to help occupy the court.

And those occupations of his years at court will gain

D

significance later. But they were far from being his
only pursuits.

Two years after his connexion with the court he
was again in France, this time with John of Gaunt on
a raid in Picardy. More than once, too, he was early
sent on missions across the Channel—once, two years
after he became an Esquire, to pass from Dover, with
two hackneys and £10 in foreign money, to an unnamed and still unknown destination; once, in highly
distinguished company, to Paris and Montreuil, to
negotiate a treaty of peace, and to treat for the marriage of Prince Richard, later Richard II, to Princess
Marie of France; and again, half a dozen times, on
other diplomatic missions. The intimate associations
of Chaucer's early life were with a French-speaking
court, and, at intervals, with France.

For the language of the English court until the
close of Chaucer's life was French. Three or four
times in Froissart Edward III speaks or is spoken
to in English, but the instances are exceptional.
When Philippa of Lancaster, the daughter of John of
Gaunt, married the King of Portugal, she introduced
French into her Portuguese court, 'as the courtly language of her English home.' '[Chaucer's] wife', as
Professor Kittredge once concisely put it, 'who came
of a French-speaking family and had been attached
to the household of a French-speaking queen, was
quite as much at home in French as in English'. That
French-speaking queen was Philippa of Hainault, the
wife of Edward III, and the Countess of Ulster had
also been brought up by her. Chaucer had breathed

a French atmosphere from the first. And it was the
poetry of France and not of England which was read
in the courtly circles in which he moved. Even his
Kentish friend John Gower wrote in French not only
half a hundred *balades* but also one of his three long
poems. And that Chaucer himself wrote in English
rather than, as he might well have done, in French,
is one of his chief glories. But in 1373 another powerful factor entered his career.

For in December 1372, about five years after he
became a member of the royal household, Chaucer
was sent to Italy, with two other commissioners, both
Genoese, to treat with the Doge of Genoa, his Council,
and the Genoese citizens regarding the establishment
in England of a port of entry for Genoese merchants,
including the franchises, liberties, immunities, and
privileges pertaining to it—a task which demanded
both keen wits and legal knowledge. And he was also
to conduct at Florence certain secret business of the
King. He was away, as his scrupulously kept accounts
record, 174 days, a week and a day under six months.
How long a time he actually spent in Italy, conditions
of travel in the fourteenth century make it hazardous
to say. But however long or short his sojourn was, it
was assuredly not of a piece with another great poet's
sedate and leisured progress later from city to city,
'contracting intimacies', as he says, 'with many persons of rank and learning, and becoming a constant
attendant at their literary parties'. Chaucer went to
Italy not, like Milton, for the purpose of consciously
rounding out a well-laid scheme of self-improvement,

but in order to conduct the business of the King. And the character of his sojourn was determined by that fact.

But he was neither blind nor dull of apprehension, and both in Genoa and (pre-eminently) in Florence he found himself in an environment intellectually kindling in the highest degree. To a citizen of guild-governed London in particular the mere outward and visible signs of the magnificence and power of the great Florentine guilds could not but be in itself a provocative experience. Dante had been fifty-one years dead, but his memory still pervaded Florence, and Petrarch had still two, Boccaccio three years to live. Giotto's campanile already stood beside Santa Maria del Fiore, though Brunelleschi's dome had not yet soared above it. The atmosphere of Florence was perennially electrical, and Italy was even then what James Howell two centuries later was to call it, 'that great limbec of working brains'. Whom Chaucer may have actually met in Florence is matter for conjecture only. The point of prime importance is the fact that when he returned to England he carried with him manuscripts of Dante, Boccaccio, and Petrarch. His own particular and private Renaissance had begun, and the demand (unsuccessful, as it happened) of Genoese merchants for a port in England changed the current of English poetry.

In 1374 Chaucer was appointed Controller of the Customs and Subsidies on wools, hides, and wool-fells in the port of London, and also, for the latter part of the period, Controller as well of Petty Customs on 'wine, cloths, and other customable merchandise'. And for twelve years, no longer in Westminster but in the City, he was employed in the duties of these singularly uninspiring offices. But when his reckonings were done he went, as he tells us, straight to his house, and where and what that house was the extant record of its lease explicitly informs us. For during all but perhaps the last year of his Controllership he occupied, by grant of the Mayor and Aldermen of London, *totam mansionem supra portam de Algate*—the entire dwelling on top of Aldgate, with the other structures above the gate (*cum domibus superedificatis*), and with a certain cellar or buttery (*quodam celario*) beneath the said gate, in the south section of the gate. And there, ten minutes' walk from 'the quay called Wool Wharf in the Tower ward', where his more or less arduous working hours were spent, at the eastern edge of his turbulent little medieval London, high over the busy street and above his buttery, modestly stocked (until he cannily compounded it for cash) with the King's daily pitcher of wine, Chaucer for ten or eleven years lived and read—'at another boke'—and wrote. For *The Hous of Fame* and *The Parlement of Foules*, and that masterpiece which ranks next to the *Canterbury Tales* themselves, the *Troilus*, were all of them, and more besides, quite certainly written during the leisure hours of those official years. One cannot but recall *The Scarlet Letter*, which stood in similar relation to the Custom House in Salem, and remember Lamb in India House, and Anthony Trollope writing his novels on his lap in trains and on boats between visits of inspection to post offices, and Matthew Arnold inspecting schools for a livelihood. For Chaucer was not only the first great English poet; he was also the first of a distinguished line of public servants who both because of and in spite of their absorption in affairs have memorably enriched English letters.

Five years, almost to a day, after his first return from Italy, and four years after he became Controller of the Customs, he was sent again to Italy on a mission which demanded the most seasoned diplomatic qualities. For he was dispatched this time to Lombardy, with Sir Edward de Berkeley, to treat with the formidable Bernabò Visconti, tyrant of Milan—that 'God of delyt, and scourge of Lumbardye', whose death he was later to commemorate—and with Bernabò's son-in-law, the famous English freelance Sir John Hawkwood, regarding certain business touching the King's war. He was away from London just four months. And this time, I suspect, his gain from Italy came rather through a broadening of his experience of men than in additions to his precious store of manuscripts. Italy's gift of gifts to Chaucer was his discovery of Dante, Boccaccio, and Petrarch. But even brief experience of the keen, intense, and diversified life of three powerful city-states like Genoa, Milan, and Florence could not but quicken the perceptions and enrich the observation of a Londoner possessed of Geoffrey Chaucer's training and acumen.

But what he learned of life through Italy was as nothing in comparison with the experience which was still to come at home. For it was in his own London,

and now and then through business in other parts of
England, that Chaucer found his opportunity, unrivalled among English poets, for intimate knowledge of all sorts and conditions of actors in the human
comedy. And that is why the bald official records on
which I shall still further draw become precious documents in that amazing *modus operandi* whereby God
and Nature (in the medieval phrase) sometimes proceed to make a poet. And the poet of the *Canterbury
Tales* was unwittingly in training for his masterpiece
through all these years.

After his return from Lombardy, Chaucer retained
the Controllership of the Customs for eight years
more. And during those years he was concerned not
only with ledgers and commodities, but with men.
And it is highly pertinent to my purpose, even apart
from the glimpse it gives of Chaucer's London, to
consider for a moment three of the officials with whom
he had to deal. Among the eight Collectors of Customs, all of whose accounts during Chaucer's term of
office came under his personal survey, were Sir Nicholas Brembre, Sir William Walworth, and Sir John
Philipot. Each of the three, during Chaucer's tenure,
was Lord Mayor of London—Brembre four times,
Walworth twice, and Philipot once. All three were
appointed in 1380 on a commission to investigate the
finances of the realm. All three were knighted by
the King for bravery when, in 1381, Richard II, then
a boy of fourteen, met in person the leaders of the
Kentish rebels, and when Walworth struck down Wat
Tyler in the face of the formidable rebel mob. All

three belonged to the then most powerful of the contending guilds—Brembre and Philipot to the Grocers', Walworth to the Fishmongers' Guild. Brembre possessed qualities which would endear him to Chicago, for at the time of his election as Mayor he packed the Guild Hall with his armed adherents, 'crying Kill, Kill' (*Crianz tuwez, tuwez*). Philipot—'a man of jolly wit' (says Stow), as was also Geoffrey Chaucer—fitted out at his own expense a squadron with a thousand armed men to drive the pirate Mercer the Scot from the Channel, and did it; built at his own expense one of the two stone towers, below London Bridge, to hold chains stretched across the river against French attack; loaned the King money for his expedition in 1382 to France; and at the time of Buckingham's expedition to Brittany, when the delay had forced the soldiers, as the old chronicles have it, to 'gage their armour for their victuals', he redeemed with his own money more than a thousand of their jacks. Walworth became a hero of romance. His figure is the first in Richard Johnson's *Nine Worthies of London*; as late as 1799 his effigy was still carried in the Mayoralty procession; and his statue may be seen to-day on one of the corner-stones of Holborn Viaduct. I am not dragging in impertinent material. During all but two years of Chaucer's tenure of the Controllership one, and for eight years two, of these powerful merchant princes and accomplished politicians were his associates. It was not alone in Flanders, France, and Italy that Chaucer had occasion for diplomacy.

Eleven years after he received the Controllership,

Chaucer was granted a permanent deputy at the Wool Wharf, and eight months after that, in October 1385, he was appointed by the King a Justice of the Peace for Kent. And the duties of his office, as rehearsed in the royal commission, occupy two and a half closely printed pages, and Latin is a compact language. Once again he was in distinguished company. For among his associates were Sir Simon de Burley, Constable of Dover and Warden of the Cinque Ports; John de Cobham, soon to be one of the lord governors of the realm; and five justices of the King's Courts. During the August following, Chaucer was elected one of the two Knights of the Shire for Kent, and so became a member of the Parliament summoned—with a French invasion threatened and a French fleet imminent off Dover or in the Thames—for 'arduous and urgent business concerning the state and the defence of the Kingdom and of the Church'. There was, however, to the relief of the Londoners—'timid as rabbits, fearful as mice', as Walsingham cruelly calls them—no invasion, and the only result of the bitter and stormy sessions which concerns us was the wanton execution of two of Chaucer's official associates, Sir Nicholas Brembre and Sir Simon de Burley. The noiseless tenor of the records upon which we have been drawing give no inkling of the turbulence and the ignoble strife of Richard's troubled reign. As for Chaucer, it is clear from his election that he had given up his residence in London, and was now a resident of Kent. And in October the dwelling over Aldgate, where he had spent at least eleven years, was leased to his friend

Richard Forester. Two months later he was suc-
ceeded in the Controllership.

For the next two and a half years, except for the
death of his wife, we know practically nothing of him.
And then, within precisely a year, he was appointed
to three of the most exacting and (one suspects) most
harassing of all his offices. And his tenure of them,
be it remembered, fell within the very period when
the *Canterbury Tales* quite certainly were under way.
On July 12, 1389, the King issued a royal patent.
'Know ye', it ran, after the usual address to the digni-
taries of the realm—'Know ye that we, through our
confidence in the fidelity and circumspection of our
beloved Geoffrey Chaucer, constitute and designate
him Clerk of our Works at our Westminster Palace,
our Tower of London, the Castle of Buckhampton',
and on through a list of seven royal manors, including
Eltham and Shene, the royal lodge in the New Forest,
the royal mews at Charing Cross—all with their gardens, ponds, mills, and enclosures. The post was one
of distinction, and the great builder, William of Wyke-
ham, founder of New College, Oxford, and Bishop of
Winchester, had held it before him. Chaucer was
given full power to impress every sort of workman,
to make arrest and inquisition, and to purvey every
conceivable kind of material—stone, timber, brick,
shingles, glass, iron, and lead being specifically named.
Of his further responsibilities I shall mention only
one, so engagingly bizarre that one turns to *Alice in
Wonderland* for its only congruous setting.

Chaucer had, in a word, to account for every item

of the 'dead stock' from the Palace, the Tower, the Manors, the lodges, and the mews, which stock was turned over to him by his predecessor, and by Chaucer in turn passed on to the next Clerk. And the two inventories are among the most diverting documents I know. The words in the close-packed lists which most frequently recur are *frangitur*, *devastatur*, and *debile*—broken, ruined, and dilapidated, or infirm. Chaucer took over and handed on, among innumerable other items, from Westminster Palace, eight pairs of andirons, of which two had broken and ruined feet; two handmills of which the winches were missing; an instrument called a ram, of which the bases were broken; various bits of a car, or chariot, made for King Edward; two little carts, of which one was rickety; seven images made in the likeness of Kings; and a little bell called Wyron. From the Tower, a tumbril of which one of the planks, one iron pin called a winch-pin, nine binding cords, and three wheels were completely ruined; one ram, of which all the equipment except one drawing cord was broken and ruined; another bell called Wyron; one hundred round stones called engine-stones; and a frying-pan. From the manors, three sieves, of which two were good for nothing; a pair of battered tankards; a decrepit wheelbarrow; a broken cable; an empty water-pipe; a dilapidated tub. And from all of them, hordes of andirons, rakes, picks, crowbars, panes of glass, bolts, nails, cords, ladles, and buckets.

Nor was the accounting for all this royal rubbish a perfunctory affair. The inventory which Chaucer turned over to his successor, John Gedney, ends with the formal statement that the said Johannes, who has properly accounted for the rest, has not yet receipted for the eight pairs of andirons and a few other items in the list. Whereupon John Gedney at once appends his official receipt for the said pairs of andirons and the few other items. But only in the laconic Latin of the documents themselves can the blooming welter of these dumbfounding registers be relished to the full.

Chaucer held the arduous Clerkship of the Works for a few days under two years, and during the first of these years he received two other onerous appointments. Exactly eight months after he became Clerk of the Works he was commissioned by the King, together with Sir Richard Stury and four others, to survey the walls, ditches, gutters, sewers, bridges, roads, ponds, and trenches along the Thames between Greenwich and Woolwich, with plenary power to conduct an inquiry, without favour to rich or poor, into the responsibility for their decay, and to compel the owners of abutting properties to make repairs. As if that were not enough, exactly four months later he was put by the King in charge of the repairs of St. George's Chapel, Windsor, which, as the royal commission bluntly puts it, was on the point of falling to the ground. And again he had full power to impress labour and to purvey materials. Meantime, since every rogue in London knew that as Clerk of the Works and rebuilder of St. George's Chapel he was compelled to carry at times large sums of money with him, he was at least twice robbed by highwaymen.

On September 3, 1390, at the Foul Oak, between
Greenwich and London, he was robbed, *par aucuns
notables larons*, of £20 (not far from $2,000 in present[1]
values) of the King's money, and of his horse and
other objects. But since he was on His Majesty's service, the money (there is no mention of the horse)
was refunded by the King. Exactly three days later
he was robbed again, apparently twice, at Westminster and Hatcham, where he was beaten and wounded
as well, and there is still extant the record of the
curiously interesting trial of the gang, of whom one
was sentenced to be hanged. And the laconic note
'Suspensus' stands written in the margin opposite.

Then came what cannot but have been a grateful
change. Just before (it would seem) Chaucer resigned
to John Gedney the Clerkship of the Works, he was
appointed sub-forester of the royal forest-park of
North Petherton, near Bridgwater in Somerset. He
owed the appointment, as Dr. Krauss has recently
shown, to Peter Courtenay, Knight of the Garter, and
an associate of Chaucer's friends, who 'was Constable
of Windsor during the entire period while Chaucer
was engaged in repairing St. George's Chapel', and
who was likewise busy making repairs. The full
powers of the chief forestership, which were ex-
tensive, and which involved not only competence to
manage a great estate but legal knowledge as well,
were delegated to the sub-forester. Chaucer held the
office until 1398, and possibly until he died. And
since the later records are consistent with his absence

[1] When this was written!

(save at intervals) from London until the year before his death, it is reasonable to assume that during this last decade of his life he spent much of the time in relative quiet some thirty miles from Bath, in Somerset. But whether or no, he was back in his own London when he died. On the day before Christmas, 1399, he leased from the Warden of St. Mary's Chapel, in Westminster Abbey, a tenement situated in the garden of the Chapel. The traditional date of his death, at an age between fifty-six and sixty, is October 26 of the next year.

What bearing, now, has all this mass of facts on Chaucer's *poetry*? The answer can be given in half a dozen sentences. The poet of the *Troilus* and of the *Canterbury Tales* was above all else a poet of *men*, and of their individualities and doings. And in English only Shakespeare has surpassed and none else equalled him in their portrayal. And even could some canny Archpoet of the Universe have deliberately set for Chaucer's benefit the stage, no combination of conditions which gave richer opportunities for observation of humanity, with its virtues and its foibles, could conceivably have been contrived. Kings, queens, princes of the blood, and nobles of every station and degree; masters of diplomacy and political dictators, in England, Flanders, France, and Italy; Lord Mayors, influential tradesmen of the Guilds, Justices, Knights of the Shires; men of law, clerks, multitudinous ecclesiastics; shipmen, and soldiers, and bailiffs and country gentlemen; carpenters and masons, and millers, and hedgers and ditchers, and unskilled labour of every sort—with all these and more, individually and in their complex relations, Chaucer through more than forty years stood at various times in close and even intimate connexion. The immortal figures of the *Prologue* and the *Tales* have their ancestry on one side in the Customs and the missions and the Clerkship of the Works and the offices in Kent and Somerset, and even in the survey of sewers, walls, and ditches along the Thames. Their roots are deep in the life which their creator lived. But their lineage lies also in the multitude of books which Chaucer, through those packed years, found time, miraculously as it seems, to read. And the two strains, in the masterpieces, are indissolubly merged.

What, now, of that reading which business, however exigent, seems never to have interrupted or made dull?

III. THE WORLD OF BOOKS

ONE thing is obvious upon the face of it. Chaucer had certainly read, and read early, the books which were current in the circles in which he moved—the books, namely, which were being read by the lords and ladies who set the fashion, and by his fellow pages and esquires who followed it. Those circles, as we have seen, were, in their tastes and their conventions, still predominantly French. We may take it, then, without question that Chaucer's earlier reading was largely, if not chiefly, in the contemporary courtly poetry of France. And we should expect to find him first responding to the influences that were in the very air he breathed; then, with enlarged experience and ripened powers, passing into richer fields, yet never wholly losing the impress of those earlier adventures among books. The sequence of Chaucer's reading followed, like that of other normal human beings, a course determined by the circumstances of his life and the maturing of his tastes. It is only in its amazing range, and in the genius which made use of it, that it is extraordinary.

Now French poetry in Chaucer's generation had fallen upon lean days. It was the ebb-tide of literature in France. The twelfth and thirteenth centuries had produced the great classical and chivalric romances, and the fabliaux, and the *Roman de la Rose*. The fifteenth and sixteenth centuries were to see Villon and Rabelais. Between these two superbly masculine epochs flourished, in Chaucer's century, the sophisticated, formal, and artificial poetry of courtly love. And by one of time's ironies the most masculine of English poets, with only Dryden as a second, lived during the years of his attendance upon princely and royal households in an atmosphere pervaded by the genteel conventions of the French love-vision poems. He read (it is obvious) the poems of the courtly vogue with mingled detachment and delight, and their glaring absurdities slipped from him like water from a duck's back. But their conventional framework provided him, as we shall see, with a medium which in his hands became an instrument of new and unsuspected capabilities. It was the French courtly poets who first wakened his muse, and they never quite lapsed from his memory. And his earlier work must be read in their light. Chiefly for that reason, then, but partly (I confess) because they exercise a certain fearful fascination even yet, I shall give in this chapter the lion's share to them. The classics and the great Italians are familiar ground.

I

Of the French poets contemporary with Chaucer three stand out above the rest not only in distinction but in popularity. Guillaume de Machaut was already in the forties when Chaucer was born, and he lived until Chaucer had been for three years Controller of the Customs. Jean Froissart was older than Chaucer by three or four years, and was still alive when Chaucer died. Eustace Deschamps was younger

than Chaucer by half a dozen years and survived him
by just six years. All three, accordingly, were alive,
and all three writing, during Chaucer's most impres-
sionable years. Moreover, Froissart, then writing
verses, had spent between five and six years at the
English court just before Chaucer became a member
of the royal household. Deschamps a few years later
celebrated in a *balade* Philippa of Lancaster, the
daughter of John of Gaunt; knew more than one of
Chaucer's friends; and sent to Chaucer himself a
poetical epistle. Machaut, the honoured and acknowledged master of both Froissart and Deschamps, had
wider fame than either. When Chaucer, aged seventeen or so, became a page, and later when he proceeded
esquire at court, the prestige of Machaut and the
memory of Froissart were in the atmosphere he
breathed. And the influence of Deschamps was exercised even more directly.

Machaut and Deschamps, moreover, were men
whose careers, in relation to Chaucer's, were of singular interest. Machaut had been secretary to that reck-
less, chivalrous, and turbulent figure John of Bohemia
who died gloriously at Crecy. He was with John when
he fought (like Chaucer's Knight) in the ice of Lithuania (*par les glaces en Letoe*) against the Khan of
Tartary, to whom Lithuania was tributary—where,
too (more ruthless than the Knight), he had 'Chris-
tianized' in one city, by the expeditious medium of
the sword, six thousand unbelievers (*mescreans*). Like
the Knight, too, he had 'reysed' (his word is the same)
in Prussia and in Russia, and like Chaucer himself

had been in Lombardy. And he celebrated in his longest poem the taking of Alexandria by Pierre de Lusignan, King of Cyprus, with whom Chaucer's Knight had been 'whan it was wonne'. Like Chaucer, too, he was in the service of three kings, but (much unlike him) was an ecclesiastic, and for the last forty years of his long life was a canon in the cathedral chapter of Rheims.

Deschamps, also like Chaucer, was poet, and soldier, and courtier, and man of affairs. Like Chaucer, he was a young esquire at court, and afterwards attached to its service. Like Chaucer, too, as now seems probable, he studied law. Like him he was sent to Lombardy, the first time (as it happens) in attendance at the marriage of that same Galeas Visconti whose daughter Chaucer's first patron Lionel later wed. He, too, was made inspector—not, to be sure, of sewers and ditches, but of the fortresses in Picardy; and he was a member of the expedition which had sent, as we saw, the Londoners scurrying mouse-like to their holes at the time when Chaucer's Parliament met. His indirect but momentous personal relations with Chaucer will meet us later. But one curious and tantalizing fact deserves at least mention. When Chaucer, in the campaign of 1359–60, was taken prisoner before Rheims and held for ransom, Deschamps was one of the defenders of the city, in which Machaut, then a canon of the cathedral, was in residence. But neither the older French poet nor the younger ever knew how near to them had been the English youngster who was to give them both a vicarious immortality.

Froissart's outward life as a cleric and a courtier was less adventurous. But neither Machaut nor Deschamps took so stirring a part in the life of the times as did he in the thronged and vivid pages of his *Chronicles*.

Behind these three contemporaries of Chaucer stand, however, two far more distinguished figures, without whom none of the trio could ever have written as he did, and whose influence, as well immediate as indirect, upon Chaucer's own thought and expression was only less profound. For the *Roman de la Rose* was one of the half-dozen books most closely woven into the very texture of his mind and art. And only through some knowledge of it can one comprehend why Machaut, Froissart, and Deschamps wrote as they wrote, and what the background was against which Chaucer saw them as he read. What, then, of this once widely and profoundly influential book?

II

Just at the close of the twelfth century, and not quite a century and a half before Chaucer himself, there was born in France one Guillaume de Lorris, of whom little but his name is known. Early in the thirteenth century he wrote what is now the first part of the *Roman de la Rose*, extending to nearly 4,700 lines. Forty years later, almost a century before Chaucer's birth, there was born at Meun-sur-Loire one Jean Clopinal ('Limping John'), better known as Jean de Meun, who was fifty years older than Dante, and who seems to have died about the year of Petrarch's birth.

About forty years after Guillaume de Lorris ended
his work Jean de Meun took it up, and beginning
where Guillaume left off, carried on this poem of less
than 4,700 lines to a length of 22,817 lines. The
vast poem that Jean left, in other words, is almost five
times as long as the poem that he found.

And now we enter another world, strange and
unfamiliar, in sharpest conceivable contrast with the
world of the Customs and the ditches along the
Thames and the cast-off lumber of Tower and palaces
—and yet a world in which Chaucer likewise lived;
which in due time he left; but of which he carried
recollections to the end. For Guillaume de Lorris
was a seer of 'such sights as youthful poets dream',
and was himself a poet of delicate fancy and sensitive-
ness to beauty. Jean de Meun, on the other hand, was
a disillusioned and caustic satirist, trenchant, ruthless,
mordant, and far more alive to human follies than to
youthful dreams. Never, perhaps, had a great work
so strange a genesis. It is—to repeat what I have
elsewhere said—as if Pope had taken it into his head
to complete the *Faerie Queene*, or as if Swift had been
seized by the fancy of carrying on the *Pilgrim's Progress* in the mood of Gulliver's fierce misanthropy.
Yet the poem is one poem, with the strange unity in
incongruity of tower and gargoyle, or of rood-screen
and miséricordes, in the vast harmony of a medieval
cathedral. And the work of Guillaume de Lorris
determined the framework, as the work of Jean de
Meun contributed to the substance, of French poetry
through almost three centuries.

What are the elements—stripped, as I must strip them, of both form and comeliness—of Guillaume's contribution to the poem?

There is first the May morning, then the dream, with the dreamer—drawn with simplicity and charm —as its central figure. There is the garden within a forbidding wall, and the wicket gate, with the portress Idleness—a damsel matched, feature for feature, and detail for detail of her dress, with the ladies of the poets through the next two centuries and more. And like the portress, the bird-haunted garden, fragrant with fennel and mint, which the dreamer enters, is the earlier counterpart of a hundred others. And dancing there, about the God of Love, whose garb is meticulously detailed, are Mirth, and Gladness, and Beauty, and Richesse, and Largesse, and Franchise, and Courtesy. I know nothing except the early Italian painting which has the same freshness and *naïveté*—a freshness unspoiled by many another later imitation. They are personified abstractions, to be sure, but in Guillaume's hands they refused to remain abstract—like Gladness, whose eyes laughed before her mouth, and Beauty, fair as the moon, beside which the other stars were but as little candles. And there in the garden, with the brooks and flowers and trees which Machaut and Froissart and Deschamps and Boccaccio and Chaucer all remembered, is a fountain springing from a basin of marble underneath a lofty pine, about which, carved in the stone, ran the legend: 'Here died the fair Narcissus'. The water was still welling up in shining waves, and at the bottom of the fountain were two crystal spheres which reflected all the forms and colours of the garden. And as the dreamer gazed, he saw mirrored in the crystals, among the other wonders of the garden, a rose-tree, guarded by a thorny hedge and all heaped with roses, and among them all one bud, the fairest that ever Nature made, that filled the air with its soft fragrance. And as he looked, he lifted his hand to pluck the bud, and as he raised his hand, the God of Love drew his bow to his ear, and the arrow of Beauty pierced the dreamer to his heart, and then, one after the other, the arrows of Simplesce, and Cortoisie, and Franchise, and Compaignie, and Beau-Semblant, until he lay prone and helpless on the ground. Then the real action of the poem begins.

The God of Love comes leaping to his prey and the dreamer yields himself, and does Love homage, and becomes his man. And Love takes out a little golden key, and deftly locks the lover's heart, and thereupon unfolds to him at length the statutes of the court of love—to Guillaume de Lorris, derived as they were from that Bible of medieval chivalric practice, Ovid's *Art of Love*, the very heart of the poem. And through his influence they coloured the French poetry of courtly love for the next two centuries and more.

How the Dreamer is left disconsolate without the hedge; how the youth, Fair Welcome, offers to bring him within the thorny barrier; how, when the hedge is passed and the rose almost attained, four lurking figures—Danger, and Evil Tongue, and Shame, and Fear—all spring to its defence; how, after further vicissitudes, Fair Welcome at last allows the Dreamer to kiss the Rose; how, thereupon, all the guardians of the Rose rise up in arms and banish the lover, and confine Fair Welcome in a tower—all that it is impossible to enter into in detail. But with the lamentations of the lover over Fair Welcome's imprisonment the work of Guillaume de Lorris abruptly ends.

But even this bald résumé can scarcely disguise its qualities. For what it did was once for all to embody in such form as the Middle Ages delighted in, the very core of medieval chivalry. And it gave to it a beauty of setting—the May morning, the shining river, the bird-haunted garden, the gracious and courtly figures —which stamped itself indelibly upon the imagination of succeeding generations of poets. For the influence of this first part of the *Roman de la Rose* was chiefly one of *form*, of the fixing of a situation and its setting, and that influence was potent upon Machaut and Froissart and Deschamps and, both directly and through them, upon Chaucer.

To this graceful portico, then, Jean de Meun, forty years after the death of the younger poet, proceeded to join his own bizarre edifice. Trenchant, when he will, but incredibly long-winded on occasion; corrosive as an acid; vivid to the limits of language, sometimes, in his realism; merciless in satire and invective —he makes Guillaume's delicate allegory the vehicle of his own cynical tirades against things as they are. Guillaume de Lorris was an aristocrat; Jean de Meun has a certain bourgeois directness and brutality. Guillaume's attitude towards woman is that of the mystic cult of medieval chivalry; Jean de Meun treats her

with the racy cynicism of the *fabliaux*. It is like
Hogarth over against Watteau.

Now so far as the *action* of the poem is concerned,
the importance of Jean de Meun's more than 18,000
lines is practically nil. The allegory moves forward
from the point where he takes it up, chiefly to afford
a pretext for the introduction of some new discussion,
new invective, new tirade. And the gist of it lies in
five tremendous monologues, loosely linked by a
rather perfunctory continuation of the plot. And the
most influential of these monologues were four. The
first is the speech of a racy friend of the lover, who,
after a few preliminary reflections on the Golden Age
as a time when, among its other merits, there was
neither marrying nor giving in marriage, settles down
con amore to one of the most terrific onslaughts upon
women ever penned, put in the mouth of a jealous
husband, and addressed to his wife. It is immensely
interesting as a human document; it is frankly scurrilous; and it is—of all incongruities—a continuation
of Guillaume de Lorris's delicate idealization of
womanly charm.

In the second monologue a personage called False-
Seeming goes off at score for a thousand lines in a
withering analysis of the hypocrisy of the mendicant
friars—a theme which Jean de Meun treats with only
less gusto than the foibles of womankind. In a third
an old harridan, La Vieille, who has taken a liking to
Fair Welcome, proceeds to rehearse to him with growing zest the chequered story of her life, and to descant
at large, with intimate detail, upon the failings of her

sex. Only the Wife of Bath herself surpasses her, and
without her the Wife of Bath had probably never
been. And then, in the last of the five great speeches,
without the slightest warning or connexion, we are
plunged into the most remarkable disquisition of the
poem. Apropos of nothing, Nature and Genius are
introduced, and for just a little short of 5,000 lines—
more, that is, than all of Guillaume de Lorris's poem
—they hold the stage. And into those 5,000 lines
Jean de Meun tumbled everything for which he had
earlier found no place—a discourse on nature and art,
more slurs upon women, an entire cosmogony, the
conflict of predestination and freewill, magic mirrors,
the significance of dreams, the degeneration of human
kind, the approach of a new Golden Age—all the
stock subjects which the Middle Ages loved, treated
without let or hindrance from any preconceived notion of pertinence. Finally the heat of the torch of
Genius brings the guardians of Fair Welcome out
of the tower, and then, with a long and somewhat
indecent allegorizing interpretation of the story of
Pygmalion and the Image, the poem ends.

I am inclined to think that there is, on the whole,
no book so thoroughly typical of the Middle Ages as
the *Roman de la Rose*—of their strange contradictions,
and their conflicting ideals; of their blind reverence
for authority, and their rebellious scepticism; of their
worship of woman, and their contempt for women;
of their ethereal idealism and their brute realism; of
their deadly monotony and their surging variety.
The *Divine Comedy* is typical, too, but every detail in

it has passed through the alembic of Dante's personality; the Middle Ages are there, but they are moulded by the compelling power of a supreme selective artist. In the *Roman de la Rose* the elements are present in something of their own warring chaos, yet pregnant with the poems of the next two centuries. It is one of the great germinal books of the Middle Ages.

And at last we may return with clearer understanding to the three poets whom we have left waiting, like the Dreamer, at the portal of the Garden of the Rose.

III

Now in Machaut and Froissart, and occasionally in Deschamps, the shell of Guillaume de Lorris's lovely fragment still survives, but its freshness and its spring fragrance and the unjaded delight in beauty which lends charm to its profusion of detail—all that is gone. A form which for Guillaume was as spontaneous as his own flowers and fountains has hardened into a convention and developed a technique. And the transformation reached its climax in the work of Guillaume de Machaut.

Machaut, whom Chaucer certainly read with pleasure, is perhaps the most baffling of the three to modern taste. He was as sophisticated as Guillaume de Lorris was (in the happier sense of the word) naïve. He was a highly disciplined artist in verse and a skilled musician besides, setting his lyrics to music, the scores of which still, in some cases, survive. His chief preoccupation (and that for us is the rub) was with the

fine-spun niceties and laboured technicalities of the
dominant system of courtly love, and of his verse a
canonical *ars amatoria* for the fourteenth century
could readily be compiled, not omitting the bead-
rolls of the secret symptoms of heroic love—changes
of colour between white, red, black, and bluish-green
(I am not improvising, but meticulously following
Machaut); shuddering, shivering, starting, paling,
flushing, swooning—'reeling and writhing and faint-
ing in coils'. For in blissful ignorance of both Machaut
and courtly love the Mock Turtle parodied in one
imperishable phrase the medieval symptoms of the
malady.

Machaut, moreover, in the greater number of his
poems, retains the dream setting, but he employs it
chiefly as a convenient device for setting himself going in his endless subtilizings and didactics upon his
master-theme. His pages are thronged with capi-
talized personifications, but Guillaume de Lorris's
caroling, dancing, gaily-robed abstractions, alive and
concrete in all save their names, have given place to
names alone, with which a clever dialectician con-
jures. I have read (if I may play for the moment the
devil's advocate) the greater part of what he wrote,
but I was usually on the trail of something, and that
took off the curse. Nevertheless, the reading had in
itself a dreadful fascination, like that which Jane
Austen must have delightedly felt in listening to the
conversation of whatever lady it may have been who
thereupon became immortal in the person of Miss
Bates. But the modern reader of Machaut who has

no Chaucerian axe to grind must, I fear, fall back for
adequate expression upon Tennyson's succint comment on Ben Jonson, who 'appeared' (as he unkindly
said of him) 'to move in a wide sea of glue'.

But that, I must insist again, is a twentieth-century
impression. The fourteenth century, especially in
France, indubitably liked its linked sweetness long
drawn out—much, for that matter, as the seventeenth
century loved *Le Grand Cyrus*, *Clélie*, and *Parthe-
nissa*, and the eighteenth century *Clarissa Harlowe*
and *Sir Charles Grandison*. There were, however,
reasons over and above a taste for tedium which rendered Machaut exhilarating to his own contemporaries, including Chaucer—as, indeed, if we let his
interminable lucubrations on love glide *doucement* (his
favourite adverb) over us, he is not without curious
interest even to-day. And since, in connexion with
Chaucer, we constantly read about Machaut, and
seldom read him, we may perhaps better understand
why Chaucer obviously liked him if we let him speak
for himself with a brevity which he, could he know
it, would deeply deplore. For I shall omit the very
things which were most dear to him—especially since
they are the very things which Chaucer also left out.
He played, for one thing, rather fascinating variations
on the dream motive, which he took over from the
Roman de la Rose. And since four of Chaucer's earlier
poems have the setting of a dream, an example or two
from among those poems of Machaut which Chaucer
certainly read with zest and used will later stand us
in good stead.

La Fonteinne Amoureuse, called in some of the manuscripts *Le Livre Morpheus*, is one of his poems upon which Chaucer certainly drew. And I shall ruthlessly dissect from its 2,184 lines the skeleton alone. Machaut, in the person of one of the dreamers, is about to fall asleep (after that fit of love-melancholy which punctually ushers in his dreams), when he is disturbed by the grievous lament of an unhappy lover in an adjoining chamber, to which lament he listens at great length, until the unknown unfortunate announces his resolve to compose forthwith for his lady a dolorous lay. Machaut instantly gets out of bed, puts on his clothes, lights a candle (always, he assures us, with his ear towards the fireplace to the right, where the window was through which he heard), takes his ivory tablets and his writing gear, and proceeds to set down, as it is uttered, the Complaint—a masterpiece which runs, in complex strophic stanzas, to 800 lines, and which tells the sad story of Ceyx and Alcyone. By the time this oral composition is concluded, one learns without surprise that it is day. So Machaut clothes and beautifies himself (*m'accesmay*) —this time presumably to leave the house, since he fastens his mantle about his neck, and in the very words of Dr. Johnson's friend who walked into the Strand, he puts his hat upon his head and—sits down again, and reads over from beginning to end the Complaint, to see if it has avoided repetitions in its rhyme groups. To his delighted astonishment, he discovers (and thus by modest indirection reveals to his readers his own virtuosity) that of the 100 eight-

line rhyme schemes not one occurs twice. He then
arises, washes his hands, and betakes himself to the
unknown's lodgings, whom he finds to be a rich and
powerful Prince. The two walk out together to a fair
park, adorned by a fountain, embellished with figures
drawn from the tale of Troy. The Prince, unaware
of Guillaume's eavesdropping, confides to him his sad
case, and begs Guillaume to compose for him a lay.
Whereupon Guillaume confesses his indiscretion, and
gives the Prince his own Complaint. The Prince,
overcome, at once leans head and arms upon Guillaume, and sweetly (*doucement*) falls asleep on his
breast. Guillaume, not to be outdone, sets himself
to think of *his* lady, incontinently nods, and cour-
teously falls asleep too. And at last, with the 1,569th
line of the poem, the dream is reached. Venus appears
with the Prince's lady; explains in 580 lines the meaning of the figures on the fountain; the Prince's *amie*
recites for her sleeping lover a Lay of Comfort, 319
lines in length, and places on his finger a ruby ring.
The two friends awake and the Prince discourses at
length on the dream, but brushes aside as a bagatelle
the strange fact that they dreamt it together, since,
as he points out, in ancient times 100 Roman senators
dreamed, all the hundred of them, one and the same
dream, as may be read at length in *L'Istoire des Rom-
maines*. All at once their conversation is broken in
upon by a servitor, who falling on his knees informs
the Prince that his dinner is being ruined ('*Sire, vostre
viande pert*') by their delay. Recalled to earth, they
proceed to the Prince's château and dine, whence

after three days of talk and revels, Machaut returns home. And one forgives a thousand lines of longueurs for the line, which O. Henry might have envied, with which the poem ends:

'Dites moy, fu ce bien songie?'—
'Tell me, how is that for a fine dream?'

Such as it is, the poem displays Machaut as narrator with his best foot forward, though it will be observed that I have omitted all the prolix subtilizings about love, which are the bulk of it. But the dream, it is clear, which to Guillaume de Lorris was the heart of his poem, has become to Machaut little more than a clever device to bring an unwontedly lively tale to its climax.

In *Le Dit dou Lyon*, which Chaucer says he translated, Machaut, having fallen asleep on the second day of April, 1342, is awakened on the third (both dates being scrupulously noted) by birds, and walks out by a river in which, as he goes, he washes his hands. This river, set by enchantment about a mysterious garden, and the magic bark in which only true lovers can ever cross it, and the bizarre landscape beyond the river, with its helpful and delectably fantastic lion, and a veritable menagerie of other beasts—all this and the fountain, and the gorgeous tent, and the Lady of the Land, constitute the setting of an adventure in the territories of romance. But any one who counts on such good fortune is reckoning without Machaut, for the sole adventure which awaits us is the privilege of listening to two long discourses upon love. But one of them, that of an old knight, 'honest and sage', is a masterpiece, and in its accounts of various types of lovers it reveals Machaut at his best. And life itself, for once, breaks into the tenuous fabric of the waking dream in the piquant dialogue, which Chaucer remembered, of that particular set of lovers who had been sent off by their mistresses to win their spurs, in hope to stand in their ladies' grace. 'See,' says one, 'there is the fellow who won the battle between Ireland and Cornwall.' 'By St. Thomas,' says another, '*he* has just come back from Damascus, Antioch, Damietta, Acre, Baruch, Sajetta, Sardinia, Siloa, The Mounts of Gilboa, Sion and Lebanon, Nazareth, Taraban, the Champ Flori and Calvary, on which God died. God keep him! If he lives, he will be a second Alexander.' 'But he *was* in Alexandria,' cries another who has missed the point, 'and on Mt. Sinai to boot.' But another still—and he it is who bears the bell—has reached in his wanderings the mysterious Dry Tree at the edge of the world, where the barnacles hang by their beaks. And the piquant account in the same discourse of the wooings of the rustic lovers nourished on milk and cheese, cabbages and beans and radishes, is not unworthy of Chaucer himself. Finally, the moral is pointed by the Lady of the Land with a nobility of thought and phrase which Chaucer recalled and made his own in one of the *Canterbury Tales*.

It is not then so strange, on the whole, that Chaucer, at least in his salad days, should read with keen interest the poems of Machaut, or that their technique should both waken his critical judgement and stir him to

F

emulation. For when Machaut forgets his tenuous psychologizing upon his eternal theme, he can and does tell a story with life-like detail. Moreover, his learning was, as his admirable modern editor once observed, both vast and superficial—the second, I am inclined to think, far rather than the first. He owed his classical lore, for example, in large degree to a huge twelfth-century allegorization of Ovid, in which he was steeped, and to which we shall come in a moment; and he loved to lend lustre to his pages by long confused catalogues of gods, goddesses, nymphs, and ancient heroes, impartially intermingled with biblical figures, and the knights and ladies of romance. And one is irresistibly reminded, as in moments of irreverence one contemplates their indiscriminate profusion, of the immortal stanza in *The Groves of Blarney*:

> There's statues gracing this noble place in,
> All heathen Gods and nymphs so fair;
> Bold Neptune, Plutarch, and Nicodemus,
> All standing naked in the open air.

At all events, Machaut's facile display of erudition could not but impress the youthful Chaucer, who was by way of becoming vastly, and far from superficially, learned himself. There was much, both in his artistry and even in his foibles, to interest Geoffrey Chaucer in Guillaume de Machaut.

IV

Froissart, like many another poet, is now delightful and again unconscionably dull. It is as if there were in him a clash between those instincts which made him a master of vigorous and graphic prose, and the conventions thrust upon him through the overwhelming prestige of Machaut. There are few more charming passages in poetry than Froissart's account in *L'Espinette Amoureuse* of his childhood— of his love for all those who love dogs and birds; of his schoolboy gifts of a buckle, an apple, a pear, or a glass-set ring to *pucelettes* who were *jonettes*; of the games that they played (a priceless list of over fifty of them), from setting a feather afloat in the wind and chasing butterflies, to sports of which only the tantalizing names survive; of how they made him study Latin, and beat him if he misconstrued; of how from a child he loved to fight, and had thrashed and been thrashed, and came home more than once with his clothes torn to bits; of how he ardently read love stories and, as he read, fancied himself in love. There is nothing in Machaut which approaches in freshness and simplicity that exquisite tissue of childhood memories. Then, with the same felicitous lightness of touch, he passes to the story of his own first love, and that, if one may not turn to the poem itself, may be read, retold with a touch of Froissart's spirit, in Sir Walter Besant's *Essays and Historiettes*.

One could wish that Froissart, when he turned to verse, had always written as he wrote in *L'Espinette Amoureuse*. But even when in his other poems he is most conventional, the stock conventions are sometimes invested with a verisimilitude and freshness which they never attain in Machaut, and even the same eternal platitudes have now and then the timbre

of a human voice, and not the accents of a personified
automaton. The setting of the dream, except in that
curious opening of *Le Paradys d'Amour*, which stuck
in Chaucer's memory, tends to slip from foreground
into background, and when, as often happens, the
ubiquitous conventions gain the upper hand, one can
usually count on coming, before hope dies, upon some
vivid flash or concrete bit of personal experience, as
in the reminiscence, in the *Prison Amoureuse*, of the
dinners and the dances and the damsels, when Froissart shared festivities with Lionel in Savoy, *en route*
to Lionel's marriage with Violante Visconti in 1388.
Hope dies completely only in his romance of *Meliador*,
of which he tells, in *Le Dit dou Florin*, how, in the
winter of this same 1388, night after night, in rain
or wind, he went from his inn to the castle of Gaston
Phebus, Count of Foix, and there in the lighted room,
when supper was spread—a very earthly paradise it
was, he says—read it aloud, six weeks before Christmas and four after. And *Méliàdor* is 30,771 lines in
length.

   And yet it was as a poet rather than a chronicler that
Froissart wished to be remembered, and so, in 1394,
as he tells us in the *Chronicles*, he had 'engrossed in a
fair book, well enlumined, all the matters of amours
and moralities that in four and twenty years before
[he] had made and compiled . . . and had this said
fair book well covered with velvet, garnished with
clasps of silver and gilt', and brought it himself from
France to England, and presented it to the King.
But when he reached England he found nobody who

remembered him (even, he says, 'the houses were all newly changed') save 'an ancient knight', Sir Richard Stury, with whom he walked up and down, talking, in a gallery before the King's chamber. And one wonders if Sir Richard, who four years earlier had surveyed the banks of the Thames with Geoffrey Chaucer, may have mentioned to Froissart the poet who just twenty-seven years before had followed him at court. But it is quite on the cards that Froissart, like Machaut, was never aware that Geoffrey Chaucer existed.

V

Deschamps and Chaucer, on the other hand, though they never met, came into extraordinarily interesting personal relations. For Deschamps somehow knew of Chaucer as the translator of the *Roman de la Rose*, and sent him by the hand of a common friend, as we shall later see, one of the most remarkable of all the twelve hundred *balades* which he composed; and yet again, on a later occasion, sent him (it seems clear) his longest and most significant poem, *Le Miroir de Mariage*, which Chaucer read with obvious delight. He calls himself a disciple of Machaut, but it is unmistakably Jean de Meun from whom his strain derives, though without (save in rarer moments) the elder poet's brilliancy and power. He is a critic, a moralist, a satirist, cold, saturnine, cynical, combining the hodge-podge circumstantiality of Mistress Quickly with the passion for autobiographical detail of Pepys. And the 3,145 printed pages of the text alone of his poems, containing 1,498 separate pieces, are a mine for the student of manners, the snapper-up of unconsidered trifles, and the antiquarian. Their virtuosity is amazing, but they have neither music nor grace nor charm. And yet I have turned over all those thirty centuries of pages—many of them more than once—upheld, to be sure, by the quest of something, yet captivated, in spite of myself, by the sheer exhaustless fecundity of the man. What Chaucer read of him, beyond the poems which were actually sent him, it is difficult to say, but the poems which we know he read—coming as they did when his powers in the one case were maturing, and in the other were at their very height—were inevitably woven more closely into the texture of his composition than the poems of either Machaut or Froissart.

The paradox of the two men's relations is heightened by the fact that Deschamps, who wantons in autobiographical data, is in this respect the very antipodes of Chaucer, than whom only Shakespeare is more reticent about his own affairs. With a vividness of phrase that rivals my Uncle Toby, Deschamps inveighs against his discomforts while with the army in Flanders—discomforts which Chaucer, with never a word, had also experienced. In the closing lines of a poetical epistle, which begins with his name and rank, Deschamps informs his readers that it was written, 'God be thanked, on the way back from Dam in Flanders, by a fire of red embers, at Arteville, in the year of grace of our Lord thirteen hundred eighty-five, in France, on the return from Flanders'. In similar fashion he ends another poem: 'Given at Champs, our mansion, through which all winds blow, by the fire in our chilly chamber, the third day of November, in the year thirteen hundred, sixty and ten, all chapped with the cold, and our poor head streaming with rheum from the smoke.' His twelve hundred *balades* deal with every conceivable subject: his military campaigns, his maledictions on the toothache, his dislike of tripe, his resentment against England, his observations on different ways of eating, his counsels of perfection addressed to kings and princes, his dislike for truffles, his lament for the misfortunes of the Church, his view on the seven liberal arts, his lucubrations on the Seven Deadly Sins. Peter's great sheet let down from heaven was not more catholic.

Or the *balade* may become a transcript of personal experience, as when, in the spring of 1384, Deschamps relieved the tedium of inspecting fortresses in Picardy (where Chaucer had been too) by a trip to Calais with that Othon de Granson whom Chaucer called the 'flour of hem that make in Fraunce'. They ride into the city, the *balade* tells us, Granson before, Deschamps behind. Two Englishmen come up and seize by the bridle the horse on which Deschamps is riding. The one says 'dogue', the other, 'ride'. '*Lors me devint*', Deschamps declares, '*le coulour bleue*'— 'then I grew livid in face with rage.' The two Englishmen make a sudden attempt at conversation. 'Goday', says one; the other, 'Comidre'—the *balade* making up in piquancy for shortcomings in precision. 'Then I', writes Deschamps, falling back for his retort upon the legend of the *Anglici caudati*, in which Englishmen like monkeys were endowed with tails—'Then I said, "Yes, I see your tail".' The exchange of amenities goes racily on through the *balade*, and in a later *rondeau* Deschamps recalls to Granson that same night which they had spent in Calais at the inn, reminding him twice over how they could not get to sleep for the biting of fleas, the crying of infants, the trampling of horses, the noise of the sea. Chaucer, too, described a night at the inn, but in Southwark, not in Calais, and the contrast between the art and spirit of the two descriptions is not without a certain relevancy to the differences between the two men.

VI

Machaut, Froissart, and Deschamps could boast a poetic ancestry of a century and a half. But there was still vigorously alive in France in Chaucer's day a group of poems the roots of which were in the soil of Greece and Rome, and which still retained, in forms metamorphosed almost out of recognition, something of the pristine vigour of their ancestry. The Middle Ages knew no Greek, but the great Latin epics, and with them Ovid in particular, were still read by the learned in the original. But in France the epics had also been made over into vast vernacular romances, and Ovid, having undergone post-mortem conversion to Christianity, had been attenuated into allegory. And the classical romances and Ovid Moralized were read by learned and lay alike. And Chaucer, in whom the tastes of scholar and layman went amicably hand in hand, read the epics and Ovid both in their native Latin and in their adopted French.

So much for the general. Now let me be more specific. The three great Latin epics, the *Aeneid*, the *Thebaid*, and the *Pharsalia*, though still accessible in the original, were far more widely known in Chaucer's century through the enormously popular twelfth-century romances, the *Roman d'Eneas*, the *Roman de Thèbes*, and *Li Hystore de Julius Cesar*, which are captivating reading even yet. And the story of the Trojan War, by way of two very early and curious pseudo-historical Latin narratives ascribed to a pair of mythical participants, Dictys Cretensis and Dares Phrygius, had undergone transformation in the *Roman de Troie* of Benoit de Sainte Maure. The *Metamorphoses* of Ovid also survived in Latin, but like the epics they too were most widely known in French, through the interminable, dull, pious and popular triple allegorization of them, the *Ovide Moralisé*, the chief human interest of which lies in the uncanny and fascinating ingenuity with which Ovid's naughtiest tales are endowed with esoteric spiritual meaning.

Now Chaucer (though I may not here give the grounds for my assertions) certainly read the *Aeneid* and the *Thebaid* in the original. But he also read the *Roman d'Eneas* and the *Roman de Thèbes*. He probably read the *Pharsalia*, but he assuredly read *Li Hystore de Julius Cesar*. Homer he could not know, but he did know the two apocryphal Latin narratives and Benoit's romance; and, being insatiable, he also read, since he had special interest in the Trojan

story, Guido delle Colonne's Latin translation of
Benoit, and Joseph of Exeter's Latin poem *De Bello
Trojano*—'Of the Trojan War'. What, then, of the
classical romances themselves ?

One of their greatest editors, M. Joly, makes a
penetrating remark. The Middle Ages, he observes,
are in reality a great child, and like all children keep
on begging for some one to tell them a new tale. And
(he adds) as one reads the classical romances, one
seems to be listening to a child who is trying to tell
over again, with a child's facile and uncurbed imagination, a story which somebody has told him. Indeed,
mutatis mutandis, the naïve and fantastic forms into
which in the negro mind the Biblical stories translate themselves—one thinks, for recent illustration, of
Green Pastures—throw curious light on the *naïveté*
with which classical story was retold in the romances.

One moves, as one reads their endless pages, between
two strange worlds—the world, on the one hand, in
which the heroes of Trojan, Theban, and Roman
story joust in tournaments in medieval armour; on
the other, an incredible world akin to that of Sindbad
the Sailor and the Arabian Nights. And their most
fascinating quality is the childlike delight with which
the marvellous is seized upon, and from it spun the
most enchanting fabrications, vying with each other
in profusion of impossible detail. For the great gods
have vanished, but wonder is perennial, as the writer
of the *Squire's Tale* surely knew. The graphically
detailed depiction of the marvellous in the romances
was one thing which, beyond all question, exercised

its fascination upon Chaucer. And even the briefest sketch of the thaumaturgy and magic of the romantic narratives will demonstrate the relief which they might offer to a tired Controller of the Customs, or a harassed enumerator of broken andirons, missing winch-pins, and stray frying-pans.

It was about definite objects—tombs, tents, chariots, armour, mantles—that the exuberant imagination of the romances most freely played. And I can gain my end no more quickly than by rehearsing a few of those inventories of *incredibilia* with which the narratives are crammed. In the Chambre de Beautés, or Chamber of Alabaster, flaming with gold of Arabia, and with the twelve precious stones which God chose as the most beautiful—the chamber in which the body of Hector was laid, on its way to the tomb—were four pillars, tall and fair, on each of which was an image, made by the art of three poets, sage doctors all of them, skilled in necromancy; and two of the images (you would think them angels of Paradise) had the form of maidens, and two the shape of youths. One of the maidens danced and tumbled and leaped on the pillar, so that it was a marvel that she did not fall; like a juggler, tossed and caught again four knives; while before her stood a table upon which yet other marvels were exhibited—battles of bears, boars, tigers, and lions; ships sailing on the sea, and fishes swimming; horned men and apes; serpents and demons, and monsters perilous. The automaton on another pillar played on twelve instruments (all named) so subtly that the heavenly harmonies and the choir celestial are not so delicious to hear. And after this prelude, upon the pavement scattered with fair, fresh, fragrant flowers, an eagle and a hairy satyr, armed with a mace which was even smaller than a *petit pain*, stage a mock tournament. In the tomb of Hector are also four pillars made (as 'l'Estoire' tells us) of stones which are apples fallen from a tree of strange report, which have lain for seven years in the River of Paradise, and have there acquired the virtue of rendering men incapable of sense and memory. And the tomb as a whole is so remarkable that Benoit stands ready to affirm without lying that neither the Emperor of Germany nor he of Spain could ever construct such another.

These are in the *Roman de Troie*, as is also the tomb of Penthesilea, like which no sepulchre was ever seen by Pliny, or by him who made the Apocalypse. And in the *Roman d'Eneas* is the tomb of Pallas, with its tubes of gold and sardonyx, conveying balm and terebinth into the nostrils of the dead. And there too is the yet more remarkable sepulchre of Camilla, with its magic mirror (retrieved from the *Letter of Prester John*), and an ever-burning lamp suspended from a chain of gold, which chain is held in the beak of a dove of gold, across from which dove, and likewise the work of magic, is an archer with drawn bow. At the least breath of air the arrow is released, the dove is stricken, and the lamp is shattered on the marble pavement. But the tomb is sealed, the archer motionless, and the lamp burns on for ever. Nor are the automata confined to tombs. In the *Roman d'Eneas*, in the hall where Aeneas and Dido sit down to dine, there grow on a vine of gold, subtly trained on a trellis of silver, grapes marvellously made of a thousand precious stones. And in the trellis are ten thousand birds of fine gold, whose least worth is the value of a city. And when the wind blows, the birds all sing, so that one needs neither harp nor viol nor organ, so sweet is the music of the birds. That is in Carthage, the walls of which are guarded by three ranks of powerful magnets, which draw the anachronistic armour of attacking forces to them, and hold its wearers helpless as flies in treacle.

The tents rival the tombs in the bewildering prodigality of their wonders. There was the tent of Calcas, which had belonged to Pharaoh, he who was drowned in the Red Sea, and which was so amazing that no one could rehearse its marvels either in Latin or in French. There was the tent of Adrastus, a phantasmagoria of decorations, of which the *pièce de résistance* was an eagle, the like of which neither King David nor King Solomon had in his pavilion, so brilliant it was with precious stones; and when the sun touched it, glowing fire poured from its beak. There was the tent of Capaneus on which was painted, among a thousand other marvels, the mappemonde, with all the realms and all the kings, and the two and seventy languages, and the *mer betée* and the *mer sauvage*. And the Red Sea too was there, with the passing of the sons of Israel, and the four rivers of Paradise, and Mt. Etna, which burns and vomits smoke.

Time would fail me to tell—and yet, like the Apostle

I am quoting, I shall nevertheless go on to tell—of
Briseida's mantle, a seamless robe, made through
necromancy and magic by an enchanter of India
Superior, and first worn by a sage poet of India;
formed from the skin of the beast called *dindialos*
(which is captured in strange fashion by the Ceno-
cephali), and bordered with fur of the sables which
dwell in the river of Paradise. And God never painted
on herb or flower such colours as the skins were
coloured with. There is more, much more, but that
perhaps is adequate. So too the steel of the hauberk
of Tydeus was tempered, and seven times put under
a spell, in one of the rivers of Paradise; his sword was
found in Babylon, and if one read the lettering, one
will see that Ninus bore it and had it made; and the
spear of Tydeus was so great that the stoutest Saxon
in all Saxony could barely carry it.

For anachronism, in the romances, runs mad riot
through the centuries, and space is no less flexible
than time. Tydeus, in the *Roman de Thèbes*, rides to
a great tower that once belonged to *Morgan la fée*
(who in the *Roman de Troie* was the mistress of Hector), which is guarded by a devil called Astaroth, the
master-constable of Hell, who is an adept in the
enchantments practised by the Sphinx. Among the
Theban heroes are knights from Germany, counts
of Venice, the Duke of Russia, Valgrin of Naples,
Faramond, Count of Valfeconde, Jonas de Montfort,
Chevelaux the Frisian, Salaciel the Jew. Nestor is
Duke of Chastellan. The smiles and kisses of the two
Theban princesses are sweeter than those of London

and Poitiers. Ates rides a horse of Castile, Tydeus a good horse of Gascony, Carioz, Duke of Corinth, has not only a grey horse of Slavonia but an English horse besides. The knights of Tydeus are garbed in rich mantles of Frise. Parthenopeus is clothed, and Creon armed, as are three thousand of Meleager's men, in the French guise. And modern readers are astonished at finding Chaucer's Theban knights equipped with Prussian shields! His contemporary readers would have been yet more astonished had he boggled at the detail.

Moreover, one finds in the romances, expressed in cruder form, those symptoms of the malady of love upon which Machaut, in particular, delicately refined. There are few extremer cases of heroic love than Lavinia's passion for Aeneas in the *Roman d'Eneas*, and the discourse on courtly love in *Li Hystore de Julius Cesar*, apropos of the *innamoramento* of Caesar and Cleopatra, is a masterpiece of analysis. And the symptoms, notably swooning, are spread broadcast through the romances. Even Cornelia, Pompey's wife, who under the code might not have expected so to suffer, swoons, as *Li Hystore* laconically and mathematically puts it, well thirty times at the departure of her husband (*se pasmu bien .XXX. fois au departir de son seignor*). And there are, in the *Roman de Troie*, at least thirty additional swoonings, not of heroines only, but of heroes too, and in the *Roman de Thèbes* not less than twenty-two. One loses count, in the forest, of specific sorts of trees. But the forest, as through the last few pages I have been endeavouring to suggest, is not without inducements to exploration. And in it one still comes, as one ranges it, here and there upon Chaucer's foot-prints.

I have dwelt, then, at such length upon Chaucer's French reading, not only because, of all that he read or remembered, it is to most of his readers least familiar, but also because it is well to be reminded that Chaucer delighted in good yarns, and was not averse himself to dream-landscapes and excursions in the garden of the Rose, and swooning lovers, and sketchy classical reminiscences, and catalogues of brilliantly diversified details, and horses, mirrors, swords and rings endowed with magic properties, and carbuncles, and pillars crowned with figures, and illusions wrought by 'thise subtile tregetoures'. And the lover of such good gifts of the gods did not, I think, find his French poets wholly dull.

VII

Nor did he find tedious his reading in Latin. The *Aeneid* and the *Thebaid* and the *Pharsalia* I have already mentioned. But it was Virgil and Ovid— especially the *Metamorphoses* (his 'owne book', he called it) and the *Heroides*—whom he knew best of all among the classics, together with Claudian's *Rape of Proserpine*. Horace and Juvenal I do not feel sure that he read *in extenso*, though he quotes scraps from both. But in the multifarious Latin literature of the Middle Ages he read copiously through his life. Much of it is far more interesting than half of what we read to-day. And as for the rest, Chaucer possessed the

same robust imperviousness to dullness which nerved
our own ancestors to listen with equanimity to seven-
teenth- and eighteenth-century sermons, and he had
besides (as they, I fear, did not) the happy faculty of
transmuting dullness into sparkling humour. And
his tastes were catholic! With an infallible sense for
racy polemics and vivid concreteness of damnatory
phrase he read St. Jerome's caustic tractate against
Jovinian on the subject of marriage and virginity.
He read and translated the fiercely misanthropic pages
of the *De contemptu mundi*, or 'The Wretched Engen-
dering of Mankind', of Pope Innocent III, which
Deschamps, less surprisingly, translated too. He gives
evidence of having read at least in—I doubt, having
tried it, whether he would read it through—the huge
work on predestination of Thomas Bradwardine, Fellow of Merton and Archbishop of Canterbury. His
own profound and lifelong interest in the problem
of foreknowledge, fore-ordination, and freewill would
inevitably have led him to it, but since (as Professor
Manly has observed) Bradwardine and Chaucer's
father had both accompanied Edward III to Germany in 1338, there may have been a personal interest
as well. Into an even more ponderous work, too, he
certainly at least dipped—namely, the three vast
encyclopaedic treatises of Vincent of Beauvais. The
works of Alanus de Insulis and Martianus Capella
will meet us shortly, together with the engagingly
naïve tenth-century Eclogue of Theodulus, in which
an Athenian shepherd, Pseustis, and a shepherdess,
Alithia of the seed of David, match against each other

G

in seventy-five quatrains the heroes and heroines respectively of the classics and the scriptures. And in a happy moment Chaucer read the twelfth-century *Speculum Stultorum* of Nigel Wiriker—the Odyssey of an ass, Brunellus, who has arrived at the sad conviction that his tail is much too short; who goes to Galen for advice, and is told by him, as a warning, the story of Brunetta and Bicornis, two cows, whose tails in a sudden frost were frozen in the ice; whereupon Bicornis, an impatient and precipitate female, cuts hers off, while the more wise and prudent Brunetta waits for the ice to melt. How Brunellus is impervious to reason, and goes to the University of Salerno for a remedy; how he is attacked on his way home by dogs, and half of his already too abbreviated tail bitten off; how he gives up in despair and goes to the University of Paris to become, as a last resort, a scholar—all that, especially as it touches the universities, is trenchant and sometimes rollicking satire, and Chaucer, who obviously read it with gusto, draws upon it for an incident in his own most vivacious tale.

But the Latin treatise which most profoundly influenced his thought was the *Consolation of Philosophy* of Boethius, which he translated, and on which he drew throughout his life. And with Boethius must be named another treatise, which, like the *Consolation of Philosophy* and Jean de Meun's portion of the *Roman de la Rose*, was one of the formative books of the Middle Ages—the commentary of Macrobius upon Cicero's *Somnium Scipionis*, Chaucer's own copy of which he called his 'olde book to-torn', and which was packed with the science and philosophy of the Middle Ages: dreams, and numbers, and the elements, and the spheres and their music, and the soul of the world and its eternity or transience, and the immortality of the human soul. And to those great plastic books must be added Jacobus de Voragine's *Legenda aurea*, and the Vulgate, and the Latin of the service of the Church, and especially of its majestic hymns.

Moreover, that 'besy gost' of his, which was 'thrust-[ing] alwey newe', as he says, led him, as we have already seen, into the fields of contemporary science —medicine, alchemy, astrology, astronomy—in all of which he reveals a mastery of detail which no mere smatterer could have acquired. The scope of Chaucer's reading, in a word, was as amazing as the range of his activities.

It is the making of Chaucer the poet with which we have just now to do, and it is with the stable bases laid for that high enterprise that I have now summarily dealt. And in these days when much that arrogates to itself the great name of poetry is the unhappy birth of shallow feeling and an unstored brain, it is worth remembering that hard-earned knowledge, both of life and books, went hand in hand with the creative impulse, or the divine afflatus, or what you will, in the art of Geoffrey Chaucer.

IV. OLD FORMS AND NEW CONTENT

WHEN Chaucer commenced poet he was saturated with the courtly poetry of France. His mind moved, keen and alert, through the mass of books which I have sketched, and since he was born a poet they stirred him to the exercise of his own powers. That those powers should find their first exercise in the contemporary French vein was inevitable. It was no less inevitable—Chaucer being Chaucer—that from the first his work should bear his individual stamp, and that, as his genius developed and his reading broadened its scope, later absorptions should follow and the earlier influences wane. And in the four poems with which this chapter is concerned it is that passage of his powers from morning into noon which lends them peculiar interest.

Like most of the poems which Chaucer (as we have seen) was reading, all four are dreams. For what the sonnet later became—a vogue which swept all before it—that the love-vision already was. And as Milton seized the sonnet, and in his hand the thing became a trumpet, so in Chaucer's hand a form upon which *rigor mortis* had already almost supervened became once more a thing instinct with life and capable of hitherto undreamed variety. The form as such, in a world where fashion 'passeth sone as floures fayre', has died again, and we cannot escape at first, perhaps, a sense of strangeness in the structure. But as we read from the earlier through the maturer vision-poems, the frame *per se* slips by degrees from consciousness, and what remains is the charm and humour of which it is the vehicle.

I

The earliest of the four vision-poems, the *Book of the Duchess*, is one of the few works of Chaucer which we can certainly date. For we know from the poem itself that it is an elegy upon the death of the Duchess Blanche, the first wife of John of Gaunt, who died of the pestilence, September 12, 1369. And Chaucer had been with John of Gaunt in Picardy on the very day she died. Froissart too, who longer than Chaucer had known her at court, writes of her with grace and feeling in *Le joli Buisson de Jeunesse*: 'She died young and *jolie*, about twenty-two years old, gay, gladsome, fresh, merry, sweet, simple, of modest bearing, the good lady whose name was Blanche.' And Chaucer's exquisite and heartfelt tribute far more than bears him out. But before that eulogy—the heart and the *raison d'être* of his poem—could be reached the conventions of courtly verse must be observed, and the elegy must assume the guise of a dream. And if for a moment Chaucer forgot that it was after all an elegy which he was writing, and let himself go at first for sheer delight in retelling the tale which had set him dreaming, I am sure that his contemporary readers did not feel his prelude to be irrelevant—nor need we.

But Chaucer, quite characteristically, was not content to accept the dream convention as an act of faith. Why *does* one dream? And what are the phenomena of dreaming which give verisimilitude to an invented vision ? Chaucer pondered the first question at intervals throughout his life, and in the Proem to the *House of Fame* enumerates fifteen different causes of dreams, including among them—but not from experience!—too great feebleness of brain and abstinence. But the accepted conventional cause of such dreams as found vent in verse was melancholy—the melancholy *par excellence* which arises from unrequited or otherwise unhappy love. The fact that one might not at the moment of composition be in love at all—witness Machaut's love-melancholy, intermittent as a quartan ague and punctually synchronous with his stirrings toward a vision-poem—that fact had nothing to do with the case. And so, if Chaucer in this instance is to account for his dream (as he does) by the fact that he sat up in bed to read a book in order to beguile a sleepless night, he must, *de rigueur*, account for the sleeplessness. And he does so as they ordered such matters in France, but with a verisimilitude so disconcerting that his commentators ever since, with an industry that must have delighted Chaucer's ghost, have vainly ransacked records for the hypothetical lady of his love.

As for the second question—how give likelihood to an imagined dream ?—Chaucer's keen observation of dream psychology is manifest from the very opening of the narrative. The book which he was reading when he fell asleep—he calls it a 'romaunce'—was, as his charming description makes clear, a collection of old tales, which included the *Metamorphoses*. And

there he found the story of Ceyx and Alcyone, which
Ovid tells in his Eleventh Book. Alcyone had lost
her husband Ceyx by death. And the dream which
in Chaucer follows, regarded as a dream, finds its
suggestion, with irrefragable dream logic, in the narrative, fresh in his mind, of that ancient loss. But
Chaucer knew also later tellings of Ovid's story. For
Machaut had told it too, in that dolorous lay of the
Prince in *La Fonteinne Amoureuse* to which the poet
had unscrupulously listened through the window.
Froissart, no less conventionally sleepless, had likewise read in Machaut the same story before he in
turn dreamt *Le Paradys d'Amour*. And Chaucer had
omnivorously read all three—the eleventh Metamorphosis, *La Fonteinne Amoureuse*, and *Le Paradys
d'Amour*—and as he retells the story the three blend
into a fresh and delightful *quartum quid* which is at
once all of them yet none of them but Chaucer.
One has only to read the tale as Ovid, Machaut,
Froissart, and Chaucer respectively tell it to see what
all the books and lectures ever written can never
show—the unmistakable, individual stamp which
Chaucer, even at this early day, set upon everything
he touched.

It one does read the four tellings of the tale together
—and it is a rather fascinating enterprise—one will find
Chaucer gleaning here and there among them with an
eager relish and a keen eye for new or telling morsels.
But we, with a wide field still to reap, may only glean
among his gleanings. Juno in Ovid, at Alcyone's
prayer, sends Iris to Morpheus to ask of him a dream

which shall bring to Alcyone tidings of her husband's fate. Froissart, for good measure, couples with Juno a baffling personage, Oleus, and names, among Morpheus's 'sleepy thousand sons', one Eclympasteyr —a name otherwise unknown in rhyme or prose. Chaucer, as Professor Kittredge once remarked, shied at Oleus, cannily dismissing him as 'som wight elles, I ne roghte who'. Eclympasteyr, on the other hand, so charmed him—and no wonder!—that he not only kept him but raised him to the dignity of Morpheus's heir. And that eye of his like a falcon's caught one of the only two mild essays at humour ('was never gentle lamb more mild') which have ever gladdened my eyes in Machaut's works—that delicious bit in *La Fonteinne Amoureuse* when Iris for the second time attempts to waken Morpheus, who has meantime gone to sleep again, and when the kindly but somnolent deity opens *un petiot*—just a tiny bit—*one* eye. That Chaucer could not resist, and he takes it. But it was he and not Machaut who was writing this poem. And so, instead of Iris's suave and urbane summons, Chaucer's messenger, unnamed but now unmistakably masculine, thus proceeds to waken Morpheus:

> This messager com flying faste,
> And cryed, 'O ho! awak anon!'
> Hit was for noght; ther herde him non.
> 'Awak!' quod he, 'who is, lyth there?'
> And blew his horn right in hir ere,
> And cryed 'awaketh!' wonder hyë.
> This god of slepe, *with his oon yë*
> *Cast up*, axed, 'who clepeth there?'
> 'Hit am I,' quod this messagere—

who then delivers Juno's message. Few things, too, of the sort are more engaging than the contrasted gifts which in the three poems the would-be sleepers offer Morpheus, of which Chaucer has decorously omitted the night-cap but retained the feather-bed. Then, the promise of gifts to Morpheus duly made, he falls at last asleep over his book, and dreams a dream so inly sweet, so wonderful, that not even Joseph who read Pharaoh's dream, nor Macrobius who wrote the dream of Scipio, would be competent to expound it. And instantly we are back in the May morning of the Garden of the Rose, save that Chaucer's birds, which in his dream awaked him, are on his chamber roof. The windows of his chamber are all of pictured glass, in which was wrought from the romances the story of Troy—of Hector and Priam, Achilles and Laomedon, Medea and Jason, and of Paris, Helen, and Lavinia; while on all the walls was somehow painted all the Romance of the Rose. And one wonders what were the pictures present in Chaucer's mind as he wrote what to us is only a catalogue of names. For the *House of Fame* makes it clear, as we shall see, that the classical romances did leave lively visual images upon his memory. And in the romances there were pictures in profusion. One recalls such details in the *Roman de Troie* as, for instance, the scene which still prints itself on the eye as one reads—the lines in which Medea, like Chaucer unable to sleep, gets up from her bed and opens a lattice, looks out at the just-risen moon, closes the window and turns sadly away, stops dead in the midst of the moon-lit room and listens, and hears the sound of footsteps retreating down the stairs. And the Lavinia who is pictured in the windows of Chaucer's dream-chamber is not, I think, the shadowy Lavinia of the *Aeneid* at all, but she who through 2,000 lines of the *Roman d'Eneas* fills the stage—that Lavinia, one scene from whose story, as told in the romance, Chaucer painted in the *Troilus* with such sweeping strokes that it stands out to the eye like a great canvas.

But what of the dream itself? The Dreamer hears a hunting horn, and promptly takes horse and joins the hunt—described as only a man who had hunted could do it—and asks a retainer leading a hound, 'Say, felow, who shal hunten here?' And with the utter irrelevance of a dream the answer is, 'Sir, th' emperour Octovien'. But that startling *non sequitur* is flawless dream psychology. For Chaucer, as Dreamer, had fallen asleep over Guillaume de Machaut, and the tale of Medea and Jason was also fresh in his mind, and in both there is casual mention of Octavian. And no less casually he now appears, and with that fugitive appearance vanishes, as in a dream he should, completely from the poem. Chaucer had not pondered on the ways of dreams in vain.

Then at once another figure from the Dreamer's recent reading appears and vanishes. The lion in Machaut's *Dit dou Lyon*, after its office as watch-dog of the garden had been capably performed, and Machaut accepted by the Lady of the Land, came prettily and humbly to Machaut, as if it were a little whelp (*un petit chiennet*), and Machaut petted it, and it submitted, and did wonders with its tail (*De sa queue faisoit merveilles*), and joined its ears (*joint les oreilles*). And so, a dream changeling, the lion, no longer a lion but a puppy, comes up to Chaucer as the hunt rides off:

> I was go walked fro my tree,
> And as I wente, ther cam by me
> *A whelp*, that fauned me as I stood,
> That hadde y-folowed, and coude no good.
> Hit com and creep to me as lowe,
> Right as hit hadde me y-knowe,
> Hild doun his heed and *joyned his eres*,
> And leyde al smothe doun his heres.

Then Chaucer would have caught it, but it fled and, like Octavian, is never heard of more.

But Chaucer had started to follow it, and in an instant he is in the identical dream landscape upon which Guillaume de Lorris entered as *his* dream began, and Chaucer has reached it by a leap of association over 9,098 lines of the *Roman de la Rose* to a kindred description. And that leads him into Guillaume de Lorris's dream-forest, and then, with another leap of memory across 13,000 lines of the *Roman de la Rose*, he sees in the forest a Man in Black, sitting with his back turned to an oak, 'an huge tree'—a young man, some four and twenty years of age, and he, piteous and pale, is composing a Complaint, and the Dreamer, like Machaut in *La Fonteinne Amoureuse*, listens as he composes. And at last the knot for which the tale is knit is reached.

For the Man in Black has lost his wife, as Alcyone in

the book read just before the dream had lost her husband, by *death*. But that we learn only later. For the Dreamer, with a touch of art which is sheer genius, is represented as a little dull of understanding. And it is through the questions which, in his gentle bewilderment he keeps asking, that the Man in Black is led on to describe, with growing fullness and depth of feeling, in a Portrait of a Lady unmatched (I think) save by Dante in medieval poetry, his lost love; until, at long last, with the final question: 'Sir . . . wher is she now?' and the answer, 'She is deed!' the truth breaks in upon the Dreamer's mind. The artifice was meant to be transparent, for Chaucer's hearers would instantly have recognized, with the line: 'And gode faire WHYTE [i.e. Blanche] she hete'—the subject of the elegy. But the subtlety of the perception that one will tell to a *stranger* what reticence or convention will withhold from a *friend*, and the astuteness of the invention of an obtuse but sympathetic listener— those are Chaucer's own. Psychological insight and adroitness in its exercise go hand in hand through the poem.

But Chaucer's mind was full of his recent reading. For he possessed, among his gifts, a memory which flashed along links of association from what he was reading to what he had read; and as he wrote, the thing that he recalled came back, trailing with it recollections, still unfaded, of this or that which elsewhere he had read. And his recollections coalesced, so that, like the tidings in his own House of Rumour, there was no longer 'one of two, but both at once'. And so now his memory, as he writes, darts back and forth like a swallow between eight of Machaut's poems. He catches the suggestion for his central situation from a love *débat* embodied in a pair of remarkable poems —*Le Jugement dou Roy de Behaingne* and *Le Jugement dou Roy de Navarre*—a *débat* which opens with a meeting in a wood between a knight whose lady has been false to him and a lady who has lost her lover by death. He takes over, with changed details and complete reversal of its application, the picturesque catalogue of lovers' exploits in *Le Dit dou Lyon* and substitutes for its preposterous climax a priceless transcript of reality—a dry sea and a name, the Carrenar or Black Lake, which had somehow travelled back along the silk-routes from the terrible deserts in the heart of Asia. And in the records of Sir Aurel Stein's most recent explorations the Khara-nor may now be seen, by the aid of photographs, within a stone's throw of Marco Polo's highway, while the ancient bed of a dried-up sea lies in the desert to the west. He recalls, too, bits from the *Remède de Fortune*, a poem on one of his own pet themes, and he weaves together close verbal reminiscences not only of these but also of *La Fonteinne Amoureuse*, and the *Lay de Confort*, and a *Motet*, and a *Complainte* to boot. And the incredible result is a poem which is pure Chaucer—so potent already is that unanalysable, individual Chaucerian idiom. One thinks—*mutatis valde mutandis*— of Coleridge's remark about certain lines of Wordsworth's, to the effect that if he had met them running wild in the deserts of Arabia he would instantly have screamed out 'Wordsworth'. Chaucer's image and superscription is on every line of the elegy. The *Book of the Duchess* is not a great poem. It is a fresh and lovely and (paradoxically, if you will) an original composition.

For such borrowing as we have been observing was no less a convention in Chaucer's century than the dreams and the recurring melancholy and the catalogues. There was no literary property at all, in the sense in which we employ the term. Deschamps could beg Chaucer to transplant him into his garden, as the highest compliment which he could ask. And Chaucer was paying Machaut precisely the compliment which Machaut on his part had paid Guillaume de Lorris, and the *Ovide moralisé* and *Boethius*. No angel with a flaming sword kept the gate of the garden of the Rose, or of the gardens of the Rose's subjects.

> Qu'il fu un temps qu'il n'estoit rien
> Qu'on peüst dire 'cecy est mien',
> Car toute chose estoit commune
> Comme le soleil et la lune.

II

Between the *Book of the Duchess* and the *House of Fame* as a whole some years had intervened, and much had happened. For the Second Book of the *House of Fame*, with its reference to Chaucer's 'rekeninges', was certainly written after 1374, when he became Controller of the Customs. From 1369, the date of the *Duchess*, until then he had been in attendance at court, had been more than once in France on diplomatic missions, and above all, in 1372, had visited Italy. And that meant for Chaucer not only six or seven more years of observation and action but also the entrance into his life of the most powerfully transforming influence which he experienced—the works of Dante and Boccaccio, and, in another fashion, of Petrarch. He had liked and admired the French poets, had played with them delightfully, and he never quite forgot them. But Dante, to borrow a comparison from Guillaume de Lorris, was to them like the moon, beside which the other stars seem but little candles. And Dante did for Chaucer what Greek a century later did for Europe. When the *House of Fame* was written its maker could draw at will on the *Divine Comedy—Inferno, Purgatorio,* and *Paradiso,* all three—and the *Convivio* as well. And what Chaucer read had to be said—impression and expression went hand in hand. 'Borrowing' is an inept and misleading word.

I suppose there could scarcely be a sharper contrast than that between Chaucer and Dante—between the austerity of the one and the other's buoyant and exhaustless zest in life; between an intensity like white flame, set over against an unrivalled lightness of touch; between a remorseless compression which packs stanzas into lines, lines into words, as contrasted with a lavishness for which Dryden's 'Here is God's plenty' is the only phrase; between a passion for the minutest, most circumstantial record of contemporary incidents, and a supreme indifference to such particulars. Dante's sense of artistic unity was as uncompromising as steel; Chaucer had been a practitioner of the loosely-linked court poetry of France. Dante, like Flaubert, was one of the inexorable seekers for the unique word; invincible patience was not one of Chaucer's gifts. Yet the two had characteristics in common. Both had the same unerring 'memory of the eye', and that sense for saliency of detail which, in Dante's case, bites like etcher's acid a picture into the memory. Both had (in Chaucer's case still latent) the gift of reading and rendering essential character through seeming accidents of garb, of gesture, of facial expression. And it was inevitable that Dante's influence should be profound. But it was effected above all, I think, through the impact upon a highly original genius of the *vivida vis animi* of a supreme creative personality. Chaucer's recollections of Dante's words are the least of his debts to him. Those are, for us, little more than hints which keep us aware of something which never found expression in words—the silent workings of the *Divine Comedy*, not unlike those of life, within or beneath Chaucer's consciousness. And in the *House of Fame* we meet that influence explicitly for the first time. But meanwhile Chaucer had been reading other books as well.

The *House of Fame* is a dream poem in three Books, with a Proem and an Invocation. The Proem is a compendium of Chaucer's curious ponderings upon that theme which had for him perennial fascination— the nature and the causes of dreams; and it closes with the confident assertion that neither he since he was born, nor any man before him, ever dreamed so wonderful a dream as he did on the tenth day of December. The Invocation harks back to the *Book of the Duchess* with a prayer to Morpheus, god of sleep and dreams, calling down blessings on those who take this dream aright, and invoking an almost Ernulphian curse upon those who for any cause misdeem it. Then, with a second explicit reference to December 10—one recalls that Machaut's *Dit dou Lyon* is also dated twice—the dream begins. Chaucer finds himself in an astonishing temple of glass, which he discovers to be the temple of Venus, and on its walls he sees graven, with Dido as its central figure, the whole story of the *Aeneid*. And the epitomized rehearsal of the epic of Rome is the theme of the First Book. In the Second, Chaucer is snatched up by an eagle and taken in a superbly narrated flight through the air to the House of Fame. And the Third Book describes both that bewildering structure and the no less amazing House of Rumour too, breaking off abruptly just as the secret of the poem is to be disclosed. Book I, as compared with the others, is perfunctory and sometimes tedious; Book II is a racy and vivid masterpiece, sparkling with humour and wit; Book III pours in a torrent of variegated and multitudinous detail through the graphic accounts of the Houses of Fame and Rumour, and their respective inmates. And the contrast between the First Book and the other two has significant, if also baffling, implications.

For the narrative of Book I, which displays in a series of pictures, abandoning epic order, the story of the *Aeneid* through the Fourth Book, and which gives to Dido's laments and suicide the central place, is written with unblushingly admitted haste. 'Hit were a long proces to telle', Chaucer remarks of the *innamoramento* of Dido and Aeneas, 'And over long for yow to dwelle'. The account of Dido's suicide is followed by a stock list of faithless lovers, drawn in part, either directly or by way of Machaut, from the *Ovide moralisé*; and then the story of Aeneas is picked up again and hurriedly brought to a close in a summary which crams the last eight books of the *Aeneid* into thirty-eight lines. The whole recital, except for its haste, is in the French vein, and Chaucer himself is obviously bored with it. It's long to tell, he declares again, of even so promising a theme as 'every tourment eek in helle'; let anybody who wants to know about them go to Virgil, Claudian, or Dante. Then all at once something happens to the poem. Down into the desert, into which Chaucer has passed from the door of the temple, swoops a great golden eagle, and from then to the end, without a tedious moment, the poem runs its swift and brilliant way. What was it that had happened?

Up to the very end of Book I, to repeat, the poem is in the French vein. Then, within forty-four lines, Chaucer draws upon the *Inferno*, the *Purgatorio*, and the *Paradiso*. In a word, when he ended Book I and began Book II, he was familiar with all three parts of the *Divine Comedy*, of which not a trace appears in the poem until Book I is within thirteen lines of its close. And from the moment when Dante's presence makes itself felt the poem is vivid with life. I wish one could know just what had happened. Had Chaucer, all the while knowing Dante, continued with growing boredom a theme which Dante (as he knew) had touched with a pen of fire? Or had he gone through Dante while a poem in process of composition waited? Or had the manuscript of Book I been lying in his chest since a date near that of the *Book of the Duchess*, with which in the Invocation it is linked, to be thriftily retrieved (for Chaucer was thrifty) as prologue to the swelling act of a new and freshly animating theme? Like little Edward, 'I cannot tell, I do not know'. I only wish I did!

Book II begins with a striking Invocation:

O Thought, that wroot al that I mette [dreamt].

And that is Dante's Invocation at the opening of the second Canto of the *Inferno*:

O mente, che scrivesti ciò ch'io vidi—
O Mind, that didst write what I saw.

What was it that Dante saw? He had told it, and Chaucer had read it, some threescore lines earlier in the first Canto:

A poet I was, and sang of that just son of Anchises, who came from Troy after proud Ilion was burnt.

And that is precisely what Chaucer too had sung in his own First Book. In a word, in that Invocation, present by no accident, he has now bound together, however baffling their relations otherwise, Books I and II, as if with hoops of steel.

But in Book II Chaucer must be carried, to fulfil his

purpose, to the House of Fame, and that, as he knew from the twelfth *Metamorphosis*, which he quotes, is set between heaven, earth, and sea, and is consequently inaccessible, save through the air, to mortals. How, then, is he to reach it? It was once more in Dante, whom he was reading with a falcon's eye, that he found the suggestion of the way.

For in the ninth Canto of the *Purgatorio* Dante saw in a dream an eagle poised in the sky, with plumes of gold and wings outspread, intent to swoop. And Dante seemed, in his dream, to be where Ganymede had been snatched up in an eagle's talons, and carried to Jove's house. Then it seemed to him that the eagle, having wheeled a while, descended, terrible as lightning, and snatched him up as far as the sphere of fire. Precisely so Chaucer's eagle, that shone like gold, first soared, then came down like a thunderbolt, and

> Me, fleinge, at a swappe he hente,
> And with his sours agayn up wente,
> Me caryinge in his clawes starke
> As lightly as I were a larke.

And Dante's lightning recalls to Chaucer a thunderbolt in a poem of Machaut, which he had read when he wrote the *Duchess*, and Machaut and Dante blend in Chaucer's thunderbolt—as if unconsciously to symbolize the passing and the coming sway.

But that is not quite all. There are few passages which Chaucer read that made so indelible an impression on his mind, and came so often back to memory, as the opening Canto of the *Paradiso*—

the canto which ushered in the supreme ascent in all literature through the seven spheres and the starry heavens and the empyrean. And when Chaucer first saw the eagle, its golden plumage

> . . . shoon so brighte
> That never saw men such a sighte,
> *But-if the heven hadde y-wonne*
> *Al newe of golde another sonne.*

And that is a line of the First Canto of the *Paradiso*:

> Avesse il ciel d'un altro sole adorno.

Chaucer and Coleridge, in so many respects antipodal, were endowed with the same insatiable appetite for books, and the same prehensile, amalgamating memory.

And there, too, in his house above Aldgate, his reckonings made, and dead for the nonce to all else, Chaucer had been reading, at times with mischievous delight, a batch of those portentously stately and solemn narratives of aerial excursions for which the Middle Ages had a curious appetite. He had read the *Anticlaudianus* of Alain de l'Isle, picking up from the Introduction as he went, with an eye that missed nothing, a telling phrase to which, years later, he gave a very beautiful elegiac turn. And in Alanus, Prudentia, having made an astounding chariot to carry her to the sky, rides up, drawn by five steeds, to learn the causes of the clouds, the gendering of snow and hail, the origin of thunderbolts; soars on to visit the planets and the Zodiac; and still on, to the heaven of heavens itself. And Chaucer, thinking (as he says) 'on Anteclaudian', sees under him, as Prudentia saw,

> . . . the eyrish bestes [the signs of the zodiac],
> Cloudes, mistes, and tempestes,
> Snowes, hailes, reines, windes,
> And th'engendring in hir kindes.

He had read, too, in Martianus Capella, *On the Marriage of Philology and Mercury*, the quaint tale of Philology's astonishing ascension—a flight by way of the galaxy, 126,000 stadia up, after the lady, with admirable caution, had lightened herself for the journey by deftly ejecting from her brain the learned treatises whose ponderousness weighed her down. And he knew almost by heart the great passage in Boethius which pictures the winged flight of thought through the heavens; and he had read in Dante's *Convivio* the striking passage about Phaethon's wild career through the galaxy. And so, when he himself, in the eagle's talons, after gentle reminder of Phaethon's folly, had reached a point above the Zodiac, and gazed beneath him, 'tho thoughte I', he gravely declares, 'upon Boëce',

> And than thoughte I on Marcian,
> And eek on Anteclaudian,
> That sooth was hir descripcioun
> Of al the hevenes regioun,
> As fer as that I saw the preve;
> Therfor I can hem now beleve.

And all the ponderous erudition of Martianus, Alanus, and the rest becomes, at a touch of irrepressible humour, light and buoyant as a feather, 'aloft in secret veins of air'.

It would be worth a dozen lectures if I could simply read, with a minimum of comment, the Second Book, like which nothing, since Lucian's *Icaromenippus*, had ever been written; and Lucian Chaucer, who would have gloried in him, could not know. Even Chaucer himself never surpassed the grasp of the potentialities of a situation, or the power of exquisitely humorous characterization, or the swiftness and lightness of touch which he displayed in that incomparable yarn. I am giving loose rein to superlatives I know, but the thing, in its kind, *is* superlative.

Few things even in Chaucer are more delicious than the irresistible contrast between the bland loquacity of the eagle, as they fly through the air, and Chaucer's replies, for the most part monosyllabic—as if a breath too much might work disaster—to the cheerful flow of conversation which the preternaturally edifying bird sustains: 'Gladly', 'Yis', 'Wel', 'Nay', 'No fors', 'What?' And no holder of an academic chair ever exerted himself with more benevolent solicitude to accommodate his learning to the capacity of his hearers.

> 'A ha,' quod he, 'lo, so I can
> Lewedly to a lewed man
> Spoke, and shewe him swiche skiles,
> *That he may shake hem by the biles,*
> So palpable they shulden be.'

And that burst of well-earned self-satisfaction follows the eagle's acute and logical exposition of the way in which words spoken on earth reach through the air the House of Fame—one of the most masterly pieces of exposition as exposition that I know—as the eagle, sublimely innocent of false modesty, also delightedly knew. I dare not yield to temptation further. It is all, as Addison said of the *Rape of the Lock*, *merum sal* —sheer Attic salt— and nought but itself can be its parallel.

The Third Book is a gorgeous phantasmagoria. Chaucer has been rapt to the House of Fame (since he *writes* about love, but *knows* nothing of it) to hear tidings of love and love's folk. Instead of which he sees and hears—almost everything else in the world that he is keen about! Never more gloriously did a poet play truant from his theme. The very word 'love', except in the phrase 'for goddes love', occurs but eight times in the 1,068 lines of the fragment. What interested Chaucer was his thronged description, racing like a torrent, of the House of Fame, and of Fame's *modus operandi*, and the no less lively account of the House of Rumour and its inmates. And no summary of the book can do it justice.

The Invocation levies once more upon that first Canto of the *Paradiso* upon which Chaucer has already drawn for his description of the eagle. But his mind, in the first 400 lines or so of the Book, is really playing, as in a dream, with recollections of his reading in the *romances*, and weaving from them a fabric like which neither Benoit, nor he who wrote the *Thebaid*, nor the maker of *Li Hystore de Julius Cesar* ever dreamed. And yet—and the commentators have been dull of apprehension in not seeing it—and yet in suggestion upon suggestion they are there. For

no one, I think, can come directly from a reading of
the great classical romances—and that is in part why
I have briefly sketched them—to the almost bewildering exuberance of the description of Fame's house
without feeling one's self in the same atmosphere,
surrounded by objects reminiscent of the crowded
and fantastic background of the medieval tales of
Troy and Thebes and Rome. There is no question
of borrowing; it is an alert and vivid imagination
moving, *sua sponte*, through a rich field of remembered imagery, which streams into new yet familiar
shapes, as a fresh and individual conception supplies
the mould.

The castle, all of stone of beryl, without pieces
or joinings; the figures—*not* the automata of the
romances, but so like them that one must look again
to be sure that they are not—the figures seated in
their habitacles, harping and piping, with the smaller
harpers sitting under them, and gaping up, and imi-
tating them like little apes; the charmeresses, and
jogelours and tregetours, behaving as if they were alive
—'Colle tregetour' (Chaucer's only contemporary in
the House) among them, at his tricks on a table of
sycamore, like that table in the Chambre de Beautés,
on which ships were shown sailing and fishes swimming, and horned men and apes; pillars sustaining
figures, like the pillars which bore the automata in
the Chamber of Alabaster; Fame's 'see imperial' made
of a carbuncle, the magical stone *par excellence* in the
old narratives; the great hall of the castle, which, like
Prester John's chapel, could dilate in all three dimen-

sions—all these, and 'many another delitable sighte', are dream-like but unmistakable reminiscences of the magnificent prodigality of marvels which still lends fascination to the romances. Chaucer's mind moved like a magnet over his reading, and his recollections fell together like iron-filings into a new yet to his audience provocatively reminiscent thing. We, alas! fail to catch the thronging suggestions, for *their* fiction is no longer ours.

The rest of the poem pours on in tumultuous movement—through the summoning in companies, by deafening blasts from the trumpets of Aeolus, of the throngs of aspirants for Fame; through the dizzy whirling of the House of Rumour; through the creeping and crowding of the rumours to escape at crevices and holes and windows, to fly—'wenged wondres, . . . Twenty thousand in a route'—to the Castle of Fame, as Aeolus blows them about. And the amazing structure of Rumour's house is again a fabric of reminiscences which have coalesced as in a dream. It lies in a valley beneath the Castle of Fame; it is sixty miles long; it is shaped like a cage made of twigs, such as one whittles for baskets, or panniers, or cages; it has as many doors as trees have leaves, and they stand open day and night; and in the roof there are a thousand holes and more. And it derives not only from Chaucer's reading but also from what he had seen and heard. Its whirling is swift as thought, with a noise like the roaring of a stone hurled from a catapult—a sound which Chaucer had heard when he campaigned in Picardy. It owes its thousand holes

to the *mille foramina* of the twelfth *Metamorphosis*,
a detail here transferred from the dwelling of Fame.
Its structure of twigs is recalled from those Celtic
wicker houses of which Chaucer, with friends in both
Ireland and Wales, could not but have heard, and
which he had probably seen. And revolving houses
belong to the stock-in-trade of romances and folk-
tales alike. But once more, like the castle of Fame,
the structure is a new creation—a fabric built, with
something of a dream's combined inconsequence and
logic, from coalescing reminiscences of reading and
experience.

Then, as Chaucer stands wondering at a house such
as in all his age he had never seen, there, close by,
appearing out of nowhere, as in a dream or in *Alice
in Wonderland*, is the Eagle, perched high on a stone.
Chaucer runs to him and implores him to wait until
he has seen the wonders of the house. 'Peter!' replies
the Eagle, 'that is myn entente'—'that is precisely
why I'm here'. Then, after impressing on Chaucer the
fact that he alone could get him into it, he picks him
up between his toes and sets him down within the
house. And instantly to Chaucer—who could not
know for a parallel that his own little stationary earth
was whirling too—the house ceases to go about. What
he saw in it, graphically rehearsed, may 'not now be
told for me'. But all at once he hears a great noise in
the corner of the hall where, at long last, love-tidings
were being told. And everybody was running thither
with all his might. Once there, they crowded upon
one another in a heap, and those behind began

to climb up on the others' backs, and trod on each other's heels, and stamped as men do after eels. Then at last Chaucer saw a man who seemed to be 'A man of greet auctoritee'—and with that line the poem, as we have it, ends.

May the rumour which the person in authority *may* have been on the point of telling—may that rumour have been the *causa causans* of the tale—some contemporary affair of common hearsay that had set Chaucer off in a poem about Fame and Rumour which, through his spontaneous delight in it, went on and on of its own impetus? That, with enticing plausibility and lack of evidence, has been conjectured. But I prefer to leave the question, without prejudice, to possible later illumination, with those other 'wingy Mysteries ... which have unhing'd the brains of better heads'.

I have dwelt on the *House of Fame* at disproportionate length because, short of the greater *Canterbury Tales*, it is, I think, the most Chaucerian thing that Chaucer ever wrote. The two remaining vision-poems have qualities lacking in the *House of Fame*, but they, in turn, lack the irresistible gusto and *élan* which, after the first Book, sweep the narrative on with the controlled swiftness of a mill-race. And I shall deal with them more briefly than for their merits they deserve.

III

I am not sure that the *Parliament of Fowls* came after, and not before, the *House of Fame*. The external evidence is not conclusive for the date of either poem. The one certainty is that both fall between the *Book of the Duchess* and the Prologue to the *Legend of Good Women*, and for my present purpose their relative chronological sequence is not of great concern. Nor are the grounds on which I am inclined to regard the *Parliament* as the later of the two of particular relevance here.

The Proem of the *Parliament* is written with a grave sweetness and a poised serenity which stand in sharp contrast with the livelier introductions, less checked by the curb of art, which in the *Book of the Duchess* and the *House of Fame* usher in the dream. It is steeped more deeply even than they in recollections of Chaucer's reading, and the reading is richer in content, and the recollections touched with a new urbanity. It opens with a rendering, deft and aptly applied, of the first axiom of Hippocrates—an early hint of that keen interest in the great medical treatises of the Middle Ages which has already met us. Then, after a fresh disavowal of first-hand experience of love, it goes on to tell how all day long Chaucer had been reading fast and eagerly in order to learn a certain thing, a book that 'was write with lettres olde'—a passage as precious for its revelation of the intentness, and fixity of purpose, and ardour with which Chaucer read, as that other record in the *House of Fame*. And so keen was his delight as he read that the day seemed but a moment. And then he names the book—'Tullius of the dreme of Scipioun'—and in eight compact and lucid stanzas gives the gist of Cicero's narrative of what Scipio saw in his dream, from a starry place above the spheres and the galaxy. Then, in the words of the first two lines of that second Canto of the *Inferno* which also provides the Invocation to Book II of the *House of Fame*, night falls. And the heaviness which has come upon Chaucer finds expression in a favourite reminiscence from Boethius. Then, weary after his strenuous day, he falls asleep and dreams that Scipio Africanus stands before him in the very garb in which his grandson had seen him in his dream. And then, recalling a beautifully apposite passage on dream association in Claudian, Chaucer wonders, with sound psychological insight, whether the cause of his dreaming of Africanus is not the very fact that all day long he had been reading about him in the old torn volume of Macrobius in which Scipio's dream was told. At last, with an invocation to Venus, recalling a stirring episode in which she figured in Jean de Meun's portion of the *Roman de la Rose*, the Proem ends. And its complex weave is seamless, and every line, whether remembered from Cicero or Dante or Boethius or Claudian, bears stamped indelibly upon it: 'Geoffrey Chaucer, his mark'.

Then follows the dream. Africanus takes Chaucer by the hand and leads him into a great walled park through a double gate, the utterly Chaucerian inscriptions on which are suggested by the words which Dante saw written over the gate of Hell. And Chaucer describes his own hesitation upon entering in a simile which owes, with complete and characteristic adapta-

tion, its unmistakable suggestion to a recollection of
that same fourth Canto of the *Paradiso* upon which
the Wife of Bath, again with her own individual turn,
drew for a vivid figure. And then, from his Arachne's
web of interwoven reminiscences, Chaucer turns to
Boccaccio.

Boccaccio and Chaucer had more in common than
Chaucer and Dante. Both had a large and urbane
tolerance of life, as contrasted with the *saeva indigna-
tio* of Dante; both had also—in Rabelais's phrase—an
invincible gaiety of spirit (*guayeté desperit*); both were
men of wide and intimate acquaintance with the
world; both were consummate masters of narrative.
Dante's influence was the deeper, Boccaccio's the
broader in its scope. But between them 'they awoke
[Chaucer]'—if I may quote the words of a master himself possessed of the same quickening power—'they
awoke him to consciousness of power that was his
own. Boccaccio, in particular, did him the priceless
service of stirring him to emulation. Here, in the
Teseide and the *Filostrato*, were new and fine and
congenial things: not unapproachable masterpieces
like the ancient classics, but works that he might
hope to equal, that he might even aspire to surpass.' And with the *Teseide* in particular he played
almost as a child plays with a new toy. It is one
of the most fascinating performances I know. In
Ariadne, in *Anelida*, in *Troilus*, in the *Franklin's
Tale*, in the *Knight's Tale* where he retells the story,
he comes back and back again to it, as if its appeal
had been so irresistible that he could not keep his

hands off whatever he began. And here in the *Parliament*, in the beautiful description of the garden, Chaucer pays Boccaccio the tribute of imitation which Boccaccio in *his* garden had paid the *Roman de la Rose.*

But no sooner has he begun upon Boccaccio's graceful stanzas than they call up to him the loveliest description of a garden that he, if not any one, ever read—the account of the Earthly Paradise through which, in the twenty-eighth Canto of the *Purgatorio*, Matilda walks gathering flowers, recalling to Dante in her beauty where and what Proserpine was when her mother lost her and she the spring. And through links of association on which I dare not dwell, there is woven through three stanzas a fabric of blended imagery to which Chaucer and Boccaccio and the Apocalypse and Dante are joint contributors. And the lines, as Chaucer wrote them, were bathed for him in an atmosphere of recollected loveliness which they still have power to evoke. Then once again, only a little later, led by a phrase in Boccaccio which Dante had used too, Chaucer's mind flashes, by way of that phrase, from the *Teseide* to another of Dante's supreme passages, that fifth Canto of the *Inferno* which tells the story of Paolo and Francesca. And he weaves into Boccaccio's list of the world's great lovers every name in Dante's bead-roll of great lovers as well. Chaucer's mind, in both the *House of Fame* and the *Parliament*, moves at will through the *Divine Comedy* with a freedom and a swift responsiveness to association which only the most intimate knowledge could give. Nor is it only purple patches that he recalls. With no discernible suggestion save its aptness a phrase of Dante will come to mind, as when— still in the *Parliament*—the modest and retiring turtle dove ends her brief but pithy speech in council with a pat line from the *Purgatorio.*

Chaucer, in a word, was living at this period in a fresh and delightful world of books, and his poems, as never before in England, but as in Spenser and Milton and Coleridge and many another since, are enriched from those quickening streams of tradition on which his own Virgil and Ovid and Dante before him had drawn. And it is from his vivid and wide-ranging memories of books, with living men and women still like shadows in the background, that he weaves these earlier book-inspired but never bookish poems, as he later wove, with his books never absent from the background, his greater poems straight from life.

But as the Dreamer (whom I have left in the garden with Venus and Priapus and Bacchus and Diana and sixteen famous lovers in a row to provide diversion) went on through the park—Africanus having, dream-like, melted from the scene—he sees the great goddess Nature seated on a flowery hill, and he tells us, in two lines, that her face and her attire were just as Alcyn had described them in his *Pleynt of Kinde.* But beneath those two guileless lines lie a restraint and a consideration kinder than most of his readers knew —or know. For in the *De Planctu Naturae,* or Complaint of Nature, of that same Alanus de Insulis whom

I

we have met before, the description of Nature's vesture and her beauty fills eighteen lavish pages of Latin
text. Chaucer's rejections are often as illuminating
as his choices, but I forbear further concrete demonstration of that statement here. One detail only of
Nature's costume demands mention. There was pictured on her garment a *concilium*, or parliament, of
all the birds of the air, the beasts of the earth, and the
creatures of the rivers and the seas. And Chaucer,
with a flash of genius, detached the birds from her
pictured robe, endowed them with human speech,
and set them down in parliament, sober and serious,
racy and ribald, to hear the rival claims of three royal
tercels to the love of a formel eagle who was the
goddess Nature's fairest work.

The royal lovers' speeches, of which Chaucer, once
more considerate, gives but the gist, last all day long,
and then the common fowls, bored and impatient,
break out in the cry, 'Have done and let us go! Come
off! When shall your cursed pleading have an end?'
—a cry so loud that the Dreamer thought the trees
would have shivered to pieces at the noise of their 'kek,
kek!' 'kukkow!' 'quek, quek!' which went through his
ears. And then, his books for the nonce all forgotten,
Chaucer lets himself go—as if in his relief at no longer
having to listen to lovers—in such a scene of exquisite
parliamentary disorder as would, I fear, have made
Alanus turn in his honoured grave. For the waterfowls, the seed-fowls, and the worm-fowls, through
their spokesmen the duck, the goose, the turtle, and
the cuckoo, debate the case of the gentles with engag

ing freedom and racily colloquial ease. 'Pees', said the goose—I excerpt bits only from their speeches—

> . . . 'pees! now tak kepe every man . . .
> I seye, I rede him, though he were my brother,
> But she wol love him, lat him love another!'

> 'Lo here! a parfit reson of a goos!'
> Quod the sperhauk . . .
> 'Lo, swich hit is to have a tonge loos! . . .
> But sooth is seyd, "a fool can noght be stille". '. . .

> 'Nay, god forbede a lover shulde chaunge!'
> The turtel seyde, and wex for shame al reed;
> 'Thogh that his lady ever-more be straunge,
> Yet let him serve hir ever, til he be deed . . .
> For thogh she deyed, I wolde non other make,
> I wol ben hires, til that the deth me take.'

> 'Wel bourded!' quod the doke, 'by my hat!' . . .
> 'Ye, quek!' yit quod the doke, ful wel and faire,
> 'There been mo sterres, god wot, than a paire!'

> 'Now fy, cherl!' quod the gentil tercelet,
> 'Out of the dunghil com that word ful right' . . .

> Tho gan the cukkow putte him forth in prees . . .
> 'So I,' quod he, 'may have my make in pees,
> I recche not how longe that ye stryve' . . .

> 'Ye! have the glotoun fild ynogh his paunche,
> Than are we wel!' seyde the merlioun . . .

But Nature, with the curt order, 'Peace! I command here', intervenes; the formel asks for a respite to make up her mind between her suitors; and with Nature's verdict that the royal lovers must await their lady's decision for a year, a song for St. Valentine's day is sung, and with the shouting of the birds as they flew away 'I wook', says Chaucer,

> . . . and other bokes took me to
> To rede upon, and yet I rede alway;
> I hope, y-wis, to rede so som day
> That I shal mete som thing for to fare
> The bet; and thus to rede I nil not spare.

And there is Chaucer's own comment on the part played by his reading in his poems.

Was the *Parliament of Fowls* meant to celebrate, as a courtly compliment, a royal wooing? That has been gravely argued in many erudite pages. But unhappily, in those pages, royal courtships have been showered upon us in embarrassing profusion, until we are now in the quandary of the formel eagle herself. May I merely name the *dramatis personae* in what is rapidly becoming a comedy in (thus far) three acts? Upon one hypothesis the four eagles represent Anne of Bohemia, who married Richard II in 1382, Richard himself, Charles VI of France, and Frederick of Meissen; on a second assumption they stand for Philippa of Lancaster, daughter of John of Gaunt, Richard II again, William of Hainault, and John of Blois; while the third proposal, which first appeared within a week after this paragraph was written, suggests as the four eagles' prototypes Richard II once more (then heir-presumptive to the throne), William of Bavaria, a third suitor still to seek, and the six-year-old Princess Marie, daughter of Charles V of France, with the negotiations for whose marriage (she died while they were going on) Chaucer himself, in 1377, was concerned. Those are the contending theories—up to date!

Like Mr. Fortune, we are not impressed. I cannot easily see Geoffrey Chaucer, courtier as well as gentleman, holding up to the exquisitely ribald merriment of the Third Estate either the King and Queen, or the King and the daughter of his own most powerful friend, or the King and the little daughter of his cousin France. For unless the eagles were *meant* to be recognized the hypothesis falls to the ground. Birds will be birds; but when (once more *ex hypothesi*) royal personages are involved a diplomatic poet will moderate the transports of his no less allegorized cuckoos, ducks, and geese. And I confess, too, that it is a little difficult to see wherein precisely lies the compliment to Richard II, the protagonist in all three theories, in the rehearsal of a wooing, the upshot of which is the lady's request for a respite of a year in which she may make up her mind between the three. The truth is, I suspect, that this gravely impassioned academic quest of postponed betrothals, at which the puzzled layman wonders, would never have been thought of had not royal courtships been seductively datable matter, and had not the poem cried out for a date. For every detail of the *Parliament*, including the year's delay, is simply and adequately accounted for, as Professor Manly nearly twenty years ago made clear, if one recognize its central situation as a conventional *demande d'amours*, treated by a poet in whose hands conventions became more real than other

men's realities; and if one further take the trouble
to observe that four times in the poem Chaucer explicitly notifies his readers that the occasion is a
celebration of St. Valentine's day. I may be wrong,
and one of the allegorizers, or some fourth or fifth to
come, be right. And some day somebody will demonstrate that the edifying eagle of the *House of Fame*
is 'moral Gower'. I am sorely tempted to anticipate
that jocund day, and state the case for their identity
myself.

IV

In the Prologue to the *Legend of Good Women*
Chaucer returned for the last time, with ripened
powers and practised skill, to the conventional framework of the vision. For when the Prologue was composed he had already written (for in the poem he
names them all) not only the *Book of the Duchess*, the
House of Fame, and the *Parliament of Fowls*, but also
the stories which we now know as the *Knight's Tale*
and the *Second Nun's Tale*, *Troilus and Criseyde*, his
translations of the *Roman de la Rose* and of Boethius,
and a lost translation of Origen *Upon the Magdalen*.
And these facts bear directly upon the poem. For its
occasion, as Chaucer (though not in *propria persona*)
states it, is the fact that he had written the *Troilus*
and translated the *Romance of the Rose*. In the one
Criseyde had been false to her lover, and in the other
Jean de Meun had flouted the notion that women
were true. But that was heresy. The God of Love,
accordingly, must take a hand, and in some way the

culprit pay a penalty. And about that central situation the charming comedy is built.

The poem is so familiar that the mere mention of it
brings back to mind its lovely setting and its story—
the May morning which called Chaucer from his book
and his devotion; the long day spent in loving contemplation of 'these floures whyte and rede, Swiche as
men callen daysies in our toun'; the little arbour that
he had—somewhere in Kent now, if only one knew
just where—benched with fresh turves, in which (for
once without a book) he falls asleep; the resplendent
vision of the mighty God of Love leading by her
hand the white-crowned, green-clad queen Alceste,
followed by a company of ladies so numerous that
Chaucer could not believe that a third or even a fourth
of their number could possibly have been in the wide
world, since God made Adam out of dust. Then the
exquisite *balade* in honour of Alceste is sung; then
silence for 'the mountance of a furlong-wey of space',
when all at once the spell is shattered by the angry
deity's stern charge that Chaucer, kneeling 'stille as
any stoon' upon the 'softe and swote grene gras'
beside his flower, had been guilty of heresy against
his law. Then follows the gracious and effective
pleading by Alceste of Chaucer's case, and finally the
penance which is the *raison d'être* of the poem—to
wit, that Chaucer shall for his offence write year by
year, so long as he lives, a glorious Legend of *Good
Women*—of women, namely, who, unlike Criseyde,
have been true in loving all their lives, and so who
are, as Cupid's saints, entitled to a *Legend*. 'And whan

this book is maad,' Alceste concludes, 'yive hit the quene, On my behalfe, at Eltham or at Shene.' And with the God of Love's injunction that Chaucer put in his Legend not only Alceste but all the other ladies sitting there—saving some twenty thousand, good women all, and true of love, about whom the God admits that Chaucer may not know—and with the further mandate that Cleopatra head a list in which Medea also holds an honoured place, the Prologue ends.

I may only sketch with the utmost brevity two of the questions raised and answered by this delightful and provocative poem. Chaucer, in a graceful passage, appeals to the other poets who 'can make of sentement'—who write, that is, verse about love—to help him, and then charmingly informs them that he has already availed himself of their aid.

> Ye lovers, that can make of sentement;
> In this cas oghte ye be diligent
> To forthren me somwhat in my labour,
> Whether ye ben with the leef or with the flour.
> For wel I wot, that ye han her-biforn
> Of making ropen, and lad awey the corn;
> And I come after, glening here and there,
> And am ful glad if I may finde an ere
> Of any goodly word that ye han left.
> And thogh it happen me rehercen eft
> That ye han in your fresshe songes sayd,
> For-bereth me, and beth nat evel apayd,
> Sin that ye see I do hit in the honour
> Of love, and eek in service of the flour.

The full implications of that winning and explicit acknowledgement of obligation to contemporary poets went unnoticed until thirty years ago, when, on the hint of a chance phrase, Chaucer's encomium upon the daisy—'of alle floures flour'—was found to be an exquisitely woven texture of reminiscences of the Marguerite poems of Machaut, Froissart, and (unlooked for treasure-trove) of Eustace Deschamps. And when one remembers that Deschamps sent Chaucer by the hand of their common friend Sir Lewis Clifford a *balade*, composed in his most allusive and erudite vein; that in it he begged the 'grant trans-lateur, noble Geffroy Chaucier' to transplant him into his garden (where, to be sure, he modestly says he would be but a nettle); and that he tells Chaucer that along with the *balade* he is sending him some of his own apprentice work (*euvres d'escolier*)—when one recalls all that, one implication of Chaucer's acknowledgement is unmistakable. For in the Pro-logue Chaucer does indeed transplant, together with gleanings from the rest, a few slips from Deschamps's nursery. And since in the *balade* Deschamps had also asked Chaucer for a return in kind, one would like to believe—and may at least dally with surmise—that Chaucer sent Deschamps, during one of those friendly lulls which lent to the leisurely Hundred Years War a curious *Gemüthlichkeit*, the poem in which he had in part fulfilled an unwonted and flattering request.

In a dozen ways which I must here pass over, the Prologue is rich in interest, but in one respect it is unique. For it exists in two distinct versions, of which one is a thorough-going revision of the other. The

so-called B text, which Professor Skeat (to whom
Chaucerian scholarship owes perhaps its deepest debt)
designated in his great edition as the later, is now
generally accepted, on grounds which I may not
repeat here, as the earlier—a conclusion in which
Skeat himself, not long before his death, unreservedly
acquiesced. And there are few more fascinating and
illuminating studies in poetic technique—and in
Geoffrey Chaucer—than that which a comparison of
the two texts affords. In view of the Prologue's relation to Deschamps it is clear that the date of the
earlier version is contingent upon the date of an
opportunity for Clifford to bring to Chaucer across
the Channel, while war was going on, the parcel of
poems from Deschamps. And there is reason to fix
that opportunity in 1386, soon after Chaucer had
taken up his residence in Kent.

That the revision follows the death of Queen Anne
on June 7, 1394, is clear, and that for a strange but
conclusive reason. The *Legend* had been dedicated
to her:

> And whan this book is maad, yive hit the quene,
> On my behalfe, at Eltham, *or at Shene.*

And it was at the manor of Sheen—of which Chaucer
himself, just three years before, had been still, as
Clerk of the Works, in charge—that Anne died. She
was less than a month over twenty-eight years of age,
and Richard, six months younger, whose self-control
was never stable, in his passionate grief ordered the
manor, as contemporary chronicles record, to be
utterly demolished (*funditus mandavit et fecit extir-*

pari). The mandate was never fully carried out, though the manor was dismantled and abandoned, but of the King's intense aversion to it, after the Queen's death, the evidence is decisive. And whether by royal command, or upon Chaucer's own volition, the dedicatory couplet, with its explicit mention of the fatal palace, the very name of which Richard would have had blotted out, was expunged. Chaucer, however, seized the occasion to return to and recast his poem with an art matured by the lapse of almost if not quite the Horatian nine years. And the shift in his interests, as shown in his omissions and additions —the excision (to name no more) of a charming cento of reminiscences of the *Roman de la Rose*, and the inclusion instead, in a priceless record of Chaucer's 'sixty bokes', of Jerome against Jovinian—that, and the fuller mastery of his technique, unite in bearing out the evidence of the cancelled dedication.

The Legends themselves must have short shrift. There are nine of them, the last unfinished. *If* the work was begun in 1386, and *if* Alceste's injunction veiled an actual command, there *is* one legend for each of the nine years between 1386 and 1394. That may or may not be chance, and the case is one which calls for suspended judgement. But no one, I think, can read the Legends without perceiving that the repetition, by choice or mandate, of the same set theme grew more and more perfunctory as it advanced, until in the last Legend to be completed Chaucer makes no bones of thrice declaring, with devastating frankness, that he is overfed (*agroted*) with writing about faithless lovers, and even calls with something not remote from irritation upon God himself for grace to 'performe' (the suggestive word is his) his Legend. The delightful Prologue he had written *con amore*, but Fra Lippo Lippi's 'saints and saints And saints again' expresses, with a difference, his growing boredom with the long-drawn execution of his 'Seintes Legende of Cupyde'. One cannot wonder, for the superb *Troilus* already lay behind him and the *Canterbury Tales* were under way. And to the *Troilus* we must now turn back.

V. THE MASTERED ART

*T*ROILUS AND CRISEYDE is not only the first great poem in English, it is also, independently of period or language, one of the very great and beautiful poems of the world. But to most readers of poetry, deterred from it by that 'chaunge in forme of speche' of which Chaucer wrote, it remains a garden barred. And in fewer words than I wish I might give it, I shall try to sketch some of the elements both of its greatness and of its charm.

Like most of the great poems it tells a story, and its story, like theirs, is not invented *de novo* by the poet, but has come down to him through centuries, growing and deepening in content and import as it came, and shifting, chameleon-like, its colour with its periods and its narrators. And the story which Chaucer tells has its *fons et origo* in a medieval list of names, part of the strange detritus from that disintegration which went on through the Dark Ages, of the 'tale of Troy divine'. None of the great stories has had a more singular genesis, but I shall strip its history, in the telling, of all but the bare essentials.

I

The germ of the story lay in a crude sixth-century Latin narrative of the fall of Troy, and it reached its consummation through three strokes of genius. In the History of the Destruction of Troy—the *De Excidio Trojae Historia*—of Dares Phrygius, which

purports to be the work of a Trojan eyewitness, occurs
a long list, with summary descriptions, of the Greek
and Trojan heroes and heroines. And among them
are Troilus, Briseida, and Diomede. It was these three
portraits which set the story going, and here, translated literally, are their bald details. Troilus is big,
handsome, strong for his age, brave, eager for fame
of valour. Briseida is graceful, not tall, of fair complexion, with soft golden hair, eyebrows that joined
(*superciliis junctis*), lovely eyes, and well proportioned
form; she is smooth-tongued, friendly, modest, in-
genuous, dutiful. Diomede is brave, squarely built
(*quadratum*), big of body and stern of face, fierce in
battle, apt to brawl, hot-headed (*cerebro calido*), im-
petuous, rash. And for six centuries these *nominum
umbrae*, to which forms and attributes, no more, had
been attached, lay waiting in limbo.

Then, in the second half of the twelfth century,
a poet who was potentially (and sometimes in fact)
a great artist, Benoit de Sainte Maure, brought the
three of them together—through what promptings
of genius no one knows—in the *Roman de Troie* and
invested them with a story. But that story, as Benoit
tells it, begins with Briseida's faithlessness and leaves
the *innamoramento* to be assumed. And it is distri-
buted, too, in a series of episodes along the course of
a poem of over 30,000 lines. But there, as it lay piece-
meal, Boccaccio, with his hawk's eye for a story, found
it; saw its rich possibilities; and in the *Filostrato* gave
to the narrative its due beginning and to its characters flesh and blood; created Pandaro; and shifted

from foreground to background the operations of the Trojan war. And then Geoffrey Chaucer went down into Italy and found the *Filostrato*. And as Benoit had seen in Dares what Dares had never conceived; and as Boccaccio saw in Benoit potentialities which Benoit had missed; so to Chaucer Boccaccio's narrative became electrical with fresh suggestion, and set him creating an English masterpiece which owes in part its richness to a lineage which has its roots in the soil of Greece and Rome and France and Italy.

Now Chaucer knew both Dares and Benoit. But it was Boccaccio, in the masterly narrative of the *Filostrato*, who gave him the story in a form which fired his imagination, and under that stimulus he handled it with a large freedom which re-created it. And figures, which in this case do not lie, will display at a glance the bare fact of that freedom of which the implications will be, in a moment, our concern. Boccaccio's narrative runs to 5,680 lines, Chaucer's to 8,239. The *Troilus*, in a word, is almost half as long again as the *Filostrato*. What, in terms other than numerical, does that divergence mean?

There is, perhaps, in the first place, no more striking exhibition of the way in which a great poet's imagination is stirred, then gathers impetus and casts off trammels, than is offered by Chaucer's dealing with the *Filostrato*. One can actually watch him, from stanza to stanza, *kindling* (to use Dorothy Wordsworth's word) as he begins; then, again and again, on the spur of some suggestion, passing with a leap of the imagination beyond Boccaccio, and weaving a richer web; then (with the effect of a splendid gesture) abandoning almost completely a support which has become a clog, and throughout the heart of the poem running his own unfettered course; and then in the end reverting—not because that unchartered freedom tires, but because his runaway poem must be brought within bounds—finally returning, still with occasional divagations, to Boccaccio's safe turnpike road. It is an illuminating spectacle, and it turns a parallel reading of the *Filostrato* and the *Troilus* into an absorbing enterprise.

Let me be for a moment quite specific. Chaucer's mind starts running ahead of Boccaccio the moment he sets pen to parchment. In stanza after stanza he will follow the text of the *Filostrato* through four or five lines, then cut loose and give rein to his own impulse for the ending. Or a stanza of Boccaccio sets him off, and for a stretch of seven of his own he goes his independent gait. Then another stanza of Boccaccio starts a sequence, this time of thirty-two stanzas of pregnant characterization, to which the *Filostrato* contributes but a score of lines. And throughout these thirty-two stanzas it is Pandarus who holds the stage. Then, after half a dozen stanzas drawn from Boccaccio, Chaucer again goes off at score in a succession of eleven stanzas of his own, again in Pandare's pungent vein. And the stanzas of Book I which still remain draw but a third of their matter from Boccaccio. More than half of Book I, in a word, owes no direct debt to the *Filostrato*. And, above all, in Boccaccio's Pandaro Chaucer has already seen, and set out to portray, the lineaments of his own immortal Pandare. Moreover, even while he is closely following Boccaccio, he will suddenly give to a line or phrase his own unmistakable turn.

'How hastow thus unkindely and longe
Hid this fro me, *thou fool?*' quod Pandarus.

And Troilus replies:

'Thou coudest never in love thy-selven wisse;
How *devel* maystow bringen me to blisse?'

And 'thou fool' and 'devel', which are Chaucer, give to the lines the racy colloquial flavour of the talk of two gay young blades. And that is one instance out of hundreds.

Then, in the two great crucial Books, the Second and the Third, out of a total of 3,577 lines Boccaccio directly contributes less than 500. Those two Books, in a word, which even alone would constitute one of the masterpieces of poetry, are in conception and in execution Chaucer's own. And they are the heart of the poem.

Then Chaucer, who sees whither his glorious liberty is tending, sets out (and explicitly says so) to finish the story in his Fourth Book. He has so far used three Books to cover the ground of 294 stanzas of the *Filostrato*. And he has, for this one Book, 319 of Boccaccio's stanzas still to go. And he obviously intended to retrench. But it was not in Chaucer to translate without creating, and so, when his Fourth Book is ended, he has not only expanded the 167 stanzas of Boccaccio's Fourth Book into 243 of his own—but he has still three Books of Boccaccio left

K

to do! Undismayed, however, and still composing
with a free hand, he gives, in his Fifth and last Book,
for Boccaccio's 173 remaining stanzas, 267 of his own.
Troilus and Criseyde, in a word, is Chaucer, no less
than *As You Like It* and *Lear* are Shakespeare.

II

That is the story of the story. Let us now, to be
clear, refresh our memory of the bare frame of the
tale itself, as Chaucer tells it. I feel in general towards
stock résumés as Pandare felt towards Poliphete, but
of this one we have need. Troilus, son of Priam, and
so a prince of the blood, sees at the Feast of the Palla-
dium Criseyde, daughter of Calchas the soothsayer,
who has fled, a deserter, to the Grecian camp. And
he falls instantly and devastatingly in love—a fact of
which at the time Criseyde knows nothing. His bosom
friend and boon companion, Criseyde's young uncle
Pandare, finds him in black despair, and extracts from
him, in a diverting interview, the confession that it
is Pandare's own niece whom he hopelessly adores.
Pandare thereupon goes to Criseyde, and in a scene
of delightful urbanity and humour, first piques her
curiosity and then tells her his news, bringing into
play all his consummate astuteness in the effort to
persuade her to be kind. He leaves her, and she sits
pondering at her window, when all at once the street
below is full of jubilant cries, and Troilus, with armour
hewn and battered from a skirmish without the walls,
rides by among the plaudits of the people. And
Criseyde still sits alone, turning over in her mind

what she shall do—with the exalted and triumphant personage whom she has just seen. And that night she dreams that a great white eagle has rent out her heart without pain and left for it another. And then the scene shifts back to Troilus.

Pandare has returned, and in an inimitable compendium of the epistolary art recommends the writing of a letter. He delivers the letter to Criseyde, and once more, with the adroitness of a finished diplomat, persuades her in the end to reply. Then he takes the reins into his own hands, and the first of the two tricks by which the goal is reached is played. Criseyde is brought, on a pretext contrived by Pandare, to the house of Deiphobus, Troilus's brother, where Troilus feigns himself sick. And at an interview by his bedside the appeal to Criseyde's pity, with Pandare's competent furtherance, wins her acceptance of Troilus as her lover; and he, his own man again, spends his days once more in affairs of arms, and his nights in thoughts of his lady.

Then Pandare contrives his second stratagem. Criseyde, invited to his house to dine, is detained for the night—and to this we shall return—by *rain*. Troilus, supposed by Criseyde to be out of town, has been hidden by Pandare in a closet with a little window through which he has watched the feast. And in the night, on the ground of a plausible appeal, which Criseyde after long demur reluctantly accepts, Pandare brings Troilus in. And with an art unsurpassed, I think, in fiction, Chaucer (as we shall see) has invested the chain of circumstances which leads

to Criseyde's surrender with the ironical inevitability
of Fate.

Time passes, and then, at the instigation of Calchas,
a decree goes forth that Criseyde shall be exchanged
for Antenor, held prisoner in the Grecian camp. And
after anguished consideration, Criseyde, rejecting
Troilus's simple and direct solution, evolves her own
plan. She will go, will practise her arts upon her
father (a sinister portent, had Troilus but seen it) and
after ten days will infallibly return. Troilus sees her
go, and sees, too, Diomede as her escort. And the
'sudden Diomede', as Chaucer styles him, lets no
grass grow under his feet. For the moment that 'he
saw the folk of Troye aweye', he begins his suit.
Then the scene shifts again to Troilus, and to the
restless wanderings and waitings of the interminable
ten days; then back again to the Grecian camp, where,
on the same tenth day which Criseyde had set for her
return, Diomede, 'fresshe as braunche in May', again
urges his suit. And Criseyde tells him that she cannot
now speak of love, but

> What I shal after doon, I cannot seye;
> But trewely, *as yet* me list not pleye.

But Diomede presses on, and next day, the eleventh
since Troilus had been left behind, he pleads his cause
so well that he steals away from Criseyde, we are told,
her sorrow's core. But Chaucer, to whom Criseyde,
though frail, is dear, will only say that though Diomede began soon to woo her, before he won her there
was more to do. Then one day Troilus sees, borne
in triumph through the streets of Troy, a coat which

Deiphebus had wrested from Diomede. And pinned on the collar of Diomede's coat is the brooch which Troilus had given Criseyde at their parting. After that, he lives only to meet Diomede in battle, but neither ever had the better of the other; and after slaying, like Saul, his thousands, Troilus falls at Achilles' hand. And his unbodied ghost, taken up to the seventh sphere, looks down with ironical laughter at the little spot of earth which he has left behind.

These are the bare bones of the story as Chaucer tells it. It differs radically from Boccaccio in its treatment of the central situation, and with that divergence is bound up, both as cause and as result, a no less fundamental change in the conception of Criseyde and Pandare. And the reason is not far to seek. For in the *Filostrato* Criseida, who is own sister (though of finer clay) to the ladies of the *Decameron*, yields herself with small tax upon Pandaro's eloquence, and simply and directly, on the crucial night, herself sends for Troilus to come to her in her own house. That is the Criseida, and that the situation, which Chaucer found in Boccaccio. But that conventional intrigue of conventional characters was too obvious to allure him. And before his Second Book has run a hundred lines it is palpable that a new Criseida is before us. And that Criseyde—a woman of infinite sensibility and charm, past mistress of all the social graces, and as quick-witted in gay badinage as Pandare himself—must be won by a subtlety and *savoir faire* to match her own. It is as a campaign, and not as the storming of an easy citadel, that from this point Chaucer conceives the conduct of the story.

That drift of the action, however, can be understood—and this is fundamental—only if we remember that in it Chaucer is following an accepted literary convention: to wit, the code of courtly or chivalric love. And under that code, until Criseyde 'falsed' Troilus, no moral issue whatsoever was involved. Judged by its tenets Criseyde, in giving herself to Troilus, was wholly innocent of wrong, and first *sinned* when she was false to him. The two inflexible requirements of the courtly code—a code under which love and wedlock were looked upon as incompatible—were secrecy and fidelity. *Qui non celat, amare non potest*: he cannot love whose love is not secret. That categorical statement is the second of thirty-one rules laid down by Andreas Capellanus in his *De Amore*, the great compendium of practice under the courtly code. And Criseyde, Pandare, and Troilus were conceived by Boccaccio and Chaucer, and were so understood by their readers, as belonging to that elder, aristocratic social order within which the *ancien régime* bore sway. There is no more effective means of clearing one's mind of cant about Criseyde and Pandare than to read, mark, and inwardly digest the *De Amore*, in which one will find a strange *mundus alter et idem*.

It is not, then, Criseyde's *virtue*, in our conventional sense of the word, which must be undermined before she yields, and Pandarus has suffered with something less than even-handed justice the obloquy attached to his name. For Criseyde thinks, Hamlet-like, a little too precisely on the event to be capable of the overmastering passion which gives all for love, and the world well lost; and Pandare's masterly dialectics are directed not against her chastity but against the wary circumspection of a woman—not a maiden but, though young, a widow—who knew her world, and knew it as a world of wagging tongues. And her first concern, as under the code it must be, was for her name—a concern which Pandare, after he had over-borne it, still acknowledged when urging upon Troilus utter secrecy:

> For wel thou wost, the name as yet of here
> Among the peple, as who seyth, halwed is. . .
> Wher-fore, er I wol ferther goon a pas,
> Yet eft I thee biseche and fully seye,
> That privetee go with us in this cas,
> That is to seye, that thou us never wreye.

The code, to be sure, is utterly self-contradictory. But the discrepancy inherent in the assumed rectitude of conduct which one is invincibly reluctant to have known is not peculiar to the canons of courtly love.

Now all this touches closely the *art* of the poem. For it is precisely Chaucer's transformation of Criseyde from the typical figure of the woman quickly won to the complex, bafflingly subtle, lovely and hesitant creature he has made which sets the two central books of his poem among the masterpieces. And the matchless figure of Chaucer's Pandarus is the child of that change. For it is Criseyde's persistent scruples, from which Boccaccio's heroine is free, which call into play Pandare's brilliant endowments.

And through that same changed conception the scenes between Pandare and Criseyde, which lend to Chaucer's narrative its intermingled piquancy and charm, are, as compared with the *Filostrato*, more than doubled in scope and vividness. The metamorphosis of Criseyde—a change at once profound and subtle—was, I think, through its implications, the greatest stroke of genius in the poem.

And it was that, once more, in large measure by virtue of the metamorphosis of Pandare which it carried with it. Pandaro in the *Filostrato* is *un troian giovinetto, D'alto lignaggio e molto coraggioso*—a *youth*, in a word, whose salient qualities are boldness and noble lineage. And he is Criseida's *cousin*. Chaucer, leaving him still young, has subtly changed his kinship with Criseyde to that of *uncle*; has endowed him with all the address of a finished man of the world; and made him, as *dramatis persona*, the mouthpiece of his own wit, wisdom, and humour. And he is immortal largely because he is so essentially Chaucerborn, as one feels that Falstaff was born, of spontaneous delight in his creation. And half the delight of his readers, in turn, lies in the racy colloquialism and shrewd wisdom and pat proverbial philosophy and dry and salty humour of which there is not a trace in Boccaccio, but which are Chaucer's own. 'If one had to give the palm to a single factor in the creation of character', to quote John Galsworthy in his Romanes lecture, 'it would be to sly, dry, humour. The sort of humour which produced the Don and Sancho, Falstaff, Major Pendennis, Becky Sharp, Sam Weller,

Micawber, Betsy Trotwood, Stepan Arcadyewitch, and Mrs. Proudie.' Why Mr. Galsworthy omitted Pandare from that immortal company I do not know; but in that list only Falstaff and Sancho Panza, *me judice*, rival him. And the exquisite flexibility of his tactics, as his diplomacy is exercised, now upon Criseyde, now upon Troilus (whose character as the conventional lover Chaucer has both ennobled and enriched) is the achievement of a master of finesse. All of Chaucer—courtier, man of affairs, and poet, with Italy and England to boot—went to the making of Pandare.

III

It is impossible, in short compass, to give more than the barest inkling of the richness of the *Troilus*. We are conscious, as the story runs its course, of a twofold background: a setting, on the one hand, within the beleaguered city—where 'Simoys . . . as an arwe clere Thorugh Troye renne[th] ay downward to the see'— of utter urbanity and grace; while, on the other hand, never for long out of consciousness, and passing at intervals sharply from background into foreground, looms the siege. And that sense of impending fate lends to the gaiety and beauty of the earlier episodes, as we recall them, a peculiar poignancy.

For there are, I care not where one turn, few scenes more wholly charming than that in which Pandare begins his campaign—the scene in which he finds Criseyde seated in her 'paved parlour', with two of her ladies, listening to a maiden reading the story of the Siege of Thebes. And the talk between Criseyde and Pandare has all the light-hearted freedom and gay colloquial ease which belongs to those happy beings only who are to the manner born. And that talk and that setting are, one suspects, the fine distillation of colloquies which Chaucer remembered, in which high-bred ladies and courtiers had played their part. The art, moreover, with which in the swift give and take of the dialogue the most fugitive qualities of unaffected, vivacious speech are caught and kept, and that in verse is a triumph of mastered technique. And second only to that scene in charm is the other, in which Criseyde, with her three nieces of exquisite names—Flexippe, Antigone, and Tharbe —goes down the steps into her garden; and there, in the railed and shadowed alleys, new benched, and with fresh-sanded paths, 'fresh Antigone the whyte'

> Gan on a Trojan song to singe clere—

a song in which Chaucer remembered not Troy but Guillaume de Machaut. And in that same garden the same night,

> A nightingale, upon a cedre grene,
> Under the chambre-wal ther as she lay,
> Ful loude song ayein the mone shene,
> Paraunter, in his briddes wyse, a lay
> Of love.

Throughout the narrative Chaucer keeps *visualizing* his action and *hearing* his talk with such power of realization that we too, as we read, see while we hear. And I doubt whether any living or earlier master of fiction has surpassed, as few have equalled, Chaucer's fourteenth-century art. I must, perforce, choose but a single instance of this intimate weaving of setting and action into one texture, and must let go the delightful talk between.

Pandare, in the morning, brings to Criseyde in her palace Troilus's painfully elaborated letter. It is early still, but Pandare (he tells her) can't sleep late in May:

'I have a joly wo, a lusty sorwe.'

'What maner windes', cries Criseyde, 'gydeth yow now here?'

'Tel us your joly wo and your penaunce,
How ferforth be ye put in loves daunce.'

'By god,' quod he, 'I hoppe alwey bihinde!'
And she to-laugh, it thoughte hir herte breste.

Then,

With that they wenten arm in arm y-fere
In-to the gardin from the chaumbre doun.

And when Criseyde declares she will not answer Troilus's letter,

'No? than wol I,' quod he, 'so ye endyte.'

Therwith she lough, and seyde, 'go we dyne.'
And he gan at him-self to jape faste,
And seyde, 'nece, I have so greet a pyne
For love, that every other day I faste'—
And gan his beste japes forth to caste;
And made hir so to laughe at his folye,
That she for laughter wende for to dye.

And whan that she was comen in-to halle,
'Now, eem,' quod she, 'we wol go dyne anoon;'
And gan some of hir women to hir calle,
And streyght in-to hir chaumbre gan she goon.

And there she read the letter, word by word, and line
by line, and put it up,

> . . . and went hir in to dyne.
> And Pandarus, that in a study stood,
> Er he was war, she took him by the hood,
> And seyde, 'ye were caught er that ye wiste;'
> 'I vouche sauf,' quod he, 'do what yow liste.'

> Tho wesshen they, and sette hem doun and ete;
> And after noon ful sleyly Pandarus
> Gan drawe him to the window next the strete,
> And seyde, 'nece, who hath arayed thus
> The yonder hous, that stant afor-yeyn us?'
> 'Which hous?' quod she, and gan for to biholde,
> And knew it wel, and whos it was him tolde,

> And fillen forth in speche of thinges smale,
> And seten in the window bothe tweye.
> Whan Pandarus saw tyme un-to his tale . . .
> 'Now, nece myn, tel on,' quod he, 'I seye,
> How lyketh yow the lettre that ye woot?
> Can he ther-on? for, by my trouthe, I noot.'

> Therwith al rosy hewed tho wex she,
> And gan to humme, and seyde, 'so I trowe.'

And the talk goes on, and finally, at Pandarus's
urgency,

> . . . in-to a closet, for to avyse hir bettre,
> She wente allone . . .
> And sette hir doun, and gan a lettre wryte . . .

> She shette it, and to Pandarus gan goon,
> There as he sat and loked in-to the strete,
> And doun she sette hir by him on a stoon
> Of jaspre, up-on a quisshin gold y-bete.

Then, as they sit there, Troilus with his men rides by, and

> God woot if he sat on his hors a-right,
> Or goodly was beseyn, that ilke day!

And Pandare cries: 'Lo, yond he rit!' And Criseyde laconically replies: 'Ye, so he dooth.' Then Pandare takes the letter to Troilus, who lay in his bed in a trance betwixt hope and despair. And Pandare 'at his in-cominge . . . song, as who seyth, "lo! sumwhat I bringe",'

> And seyde, 'who is in his bed so sone
> Y-buried thus?' 'It am I, freend,' quod he.
> 'Who, Troilus? nay helpe me so the mone,'
> Quod Pandarus, 'thou shalt aryse and see
> A charme that was sent right now to thee,
> The which can helen thee of thyn accesse,
> If thou do forth-with al thy besinesse.'

> 'Ye, through the might of god!' quod Troilus.
> And Pandarus gan him the lettre take,
> And seyde, 'pardee, god hath holpen us;
> *Have here a light, and loke on al this blake.*'

In a notable critique of contemporary fiction, published only a score of years ago, occurs this sentence: 'In exact correspondence with that ·marvellous technical power exhibited in modern French pictures of the realistic school, there has been developed in realistic fiction a fidelity, a life-likeness, a vividness, a touch, which are extraordinary and new.' And instances are given from Tolstoi and Hardy. And yet, in certain qualities which we dub modern, Chaucer was as modern as the moderns, six centuries before their birth.

Let me take but one more 'modern instance'. One

of the most effective plays of recent years is Colton and
Randolph's *Rain*, and in that, as in the tale on which
it is founded, rain assumes the relentless character of
Fate. And in the *Troilus*, rain, with consummate art, is
made the fated instrument of Criseyde's surrender. It
was raining when Pandare asked her to his house, and
she was loath to come. But come at last she did. And
when the gay supper was over she set out for home.
But the stars in their courses fought against her. For

> The bente mone with hir hornes pale,
> Saturne, and Jove, in Cancro joyned were,
> That swich a rayn from hevene gan avale,
> That every maner womman that was there
> Hadde of that smoky reyn a verray fere;
> At which Pandare tho lough, and seyde thenne,
> 'Now were it tyme a lady to go henne!'

And he begged Criseyde, as she loved him, to spend
the night. And she, 'sin it ron, and al was on a flood',
made virtue of necessity and stayed. Then the feast
went on again, until Pandare, exclaiming, 'lord, this
is an huge reyn! This were a weder for to slepen inne',
sent all his guests to bed.

> And ever-mo so sternelich it ron,
> And blew ther-with so wonderliche loude,
> That wel neigh no man heren other coude.

And in 'a tumultous privacy of storm' Pandare's last
stratagem was carried out. And in the morning, when
Criseyde, in a revulsion of feeling, greets him with her
terrible: 'Fox that ye been!' it is to the rain which has
all night kept them awake that he ironically refers.

But Criseyde's fate had been for six centuries

written in the stars. And we owe to an observation of Professor Root this heightening of our apprehension of the closeness with which Chaucer wove his web of circumstance. For the conjunction of Jupiter and Saturn in Cancer, which did actually take place in 1385, had not before occurred since 769. And 'the bente mone with hir hornes pale' was visible beside Jupiter and Saturn in May of that year. And Chaucer, who was a watcher of the skies, and who knew the almost unparalleled character of the conjunction, had prefaced his reference to it with a doubly explicit invocation of Fortune, 'executrice of wierdes [Fates]'. For the conjunction, astrologically interpreted, included in its operations floods and heavy rains. And Chaucer ends his invocation to 'the influences of thise hevenes hye' with the words: '*This mene I now,* for she [Criseyde] *gan hoomward hye,* But execut was al bisyde hir leve, At the goddes wil; *for which she moste bleve* [remain]'. And the next line ushers in the conjunction with its attendant floods of rain—the will of the gods which frustrates and nullifies her own.

So strong is destiny, wrote Chaucer of another fated incident, that

> . . . though the world had sworn
> The contrarie of a thing, by ye or nay,
> Yet somtyme it shal fallen on a day
> *That falleth nat eft with-inne a thousand yere.*

And what he has done in the *Troilus* through this (in effect) millennial portent of the skies is to make it clear past peradventure that Criseyde remained

in Pandare's house that night, to use words of a greater
than Chaucer, 'by an enforced obedience of planetary
influence', and that it was the stars which were guilty
of her disaster.

But Chaucer knew too that Fate works through
character—which perhaps is fated too. And he does
not blink the fact that Criseyde was the victim of her
own qualities. Those write who saw her, says Chaucer,
'that Paradys stood formed in her yën'. And he has
made her a woman not only of subtle brain but also
of exquisite sensibility and charm—a woman beside
whom Boccaccio's Criseida is an unlesson'd girl. But
she is also, he adds, 'tendre-herted, *slydinge of corage*':
fickle of heart—like Reuben, 'unstable as water'. But
he has made her—for she is essentially his creation—
so lovely that he cannot quite bear the fore-doomed
end of a heart that was unstable and tender at once.
And when the end has come he takes leave of her
with a compassion like that with which a father pitieth
his children:

> Ne me ne list this sely womman chyde
> Ferther than the story wol devyse.
> Hir name, allas! is publisshed so wyde,
> That for hir gilt it oughte y-now suffyse.
> And if I mighte excuse hir any wysc,
> For she so sory was for hir untrouthe,
> Y-wis, I wolde excuse hir yet for routhe.

'Poore intricated soule!' one may almost exclaim in
John Donne's words: 'Riddling, perplexed, labyrin-
thicall soule!'

The *Troilus* ends in an access of personal feeling without parallel elsewhere in Chaucer's works. I know nothing quite like the tumultuous hitherings and thitherings of mood and matter in the last dozen stanzas of the poem—the appeal, half mocking, half serious, to gentle ladies not to be wroth with him for writing of Criseyde's unfaithfulness; the touching address to 'litel myn tregedie':

> But litel book, no making thou n'envye,
> But subgit be to alle pocsye;
> And kis the steppes, wher-as thou seest pace
> Virgile, Ovyde, Omer, Lucan, and Stace.

the prayer that it may not suffer, through change of tongue, mismetring or misunderstanding; the death of Troilus, almost an afterthought, and the happy ascent of his 'lighte goost' through the spheres—an ascent which was originally Arcite's in the *Teseide*, and before that (as Tyrwhitt in a long neglected note observed) was Pompey's apotheosis in the *Pharsalia*. Then, with an appeal of almost passionate sincerity to 'yonge fresshe folkes, he or she', to repair from earthly loves to Him who for love died on the cross, and will 'false' no one, Chaucer passes, through the dedication, to the deeply reverent prayer to 'that sothfast Crist'—that *loyal* Christ—'that starf on rode', with which the poem ends:

> Thou oon, and two, and three, eterne on-lyve,
> That regnest ay in three and two and oon,
> Uncircumscript, and al mayst circumscryve,
> Us from visible and invisible foon
> Defende; and to thy mercy, everychoon,
> So make us, Jesus, for thy grace, digne,
> For love of mayde and moder thyn benigne! Amen.

L

Chaucer, when he ended the *Troilus*, was profoundly moved, and he turns, as so often at moments of heightened feeling, to the great passages in Dante, and to the Offices and hymns of the Church. And his sublime invocation is compact of both. For its opening is a word by word rendering of three lines in one of the loftiest cantos of the *Paradiso*:

> Quell' uno e due e tre che sempre vive,
> E regna sempre in tre e due ed uno,
> Non circonscritto, e tutto circonscrive. . .

And its close breathes the very spirit of the beautiful Office of the Virgin.

Is Chaucer, in the torrent of feeling with which the poem ends, repudiating his own masterpiece? No notion, I think, could be farther from the truth. He has depicted, with what he must have known to be almost supreme art, the tragic irony of life. And now the poignancy of what he has vicariously experienced, no less as a very human being than as an artist, is almost more than he can bear. It is the same revulsion which Philip Sidney experienced, looking back, in his closing sonnet, on the great sequence in which he too had depicted earthly love:

> Leave me, O love, which reachest but to dust,
> And thou, my mind, aspire to higher things!
> Grow rich in that which never taketh rust . . .
> Eternal Love, maintain thy life in me!

In the closing lines of the *Troilus*, and in the infinite pity of his farewell to Criseyde, Chaucer, one cannot but believe, has for almost the only time revealed something of his very self.

IV

When Chaucer ended the *Troilus* he was master of his art. And the crowning achievement of that art was still before him. He had begun, in the vision poems, by accepting conventional frames, and filling them, in growing abundance, with the spoils of a reading which had grown, *pari passu*, in breadth and in depth. In the *Troilus* he had found a great narrative fabric of rich content, and had exercised on both form and substance his own architectonic powers. And now, at the height of those powers, he creates for himself a structural form, flexible, and all but exhaustless in its possibilities, and draws for its content upon all the garnered reading and experience of his life. And the medium which he chose was the oldest and most universal form of entertainment in the world. But once more, in touching it, he re-created it.

One of the greatest Oriental collections of tales bears the graphic title *Kathāsaritsāgara*: 'The Ocean of the Streams of Stories'—that ocean which through unnumbered centuries has ebbed and flowed across the world, and into which, and like currents through which, the streams of story have endlessly poured. And into Chaucer's England, as into continental Europe, tales had for generations drifted along the trade-routes, and followed in the wake of the Crusades, and passed from mouth to mouth by strange and hidden ways, from that cradle and nursery of story, the *ur*-old and prolific East—from Hindustan, and Arabia, and Persia, and Burmah, and Thibet—shifting in shape and colour as they passed from land to land, but keeping their kernel, their *core* intact. And they lent matter alike to the *fabliaux* and to the legends of the saints; and to the romances they gave themes and embroidery of marvels; and they served as *exempla* in sermons; and in the *Seven Wise Masters*, and the *Cento Novelle Antiche*, and the *Decameron*, and the *Heptameron* they came together again into collections, as they had earlier been gathered in the *Kathāsaritsāgara*, and the *Pañchatantra*, and the *Thousand and One Nights*.

But the true home of stories is not in books but on the lips of men, and tales passed current from mouth to mouth in the Occident as in the East. And Chaucer, who knew both books and men, not only read tales but *heard* them. And that is a fact which, in our preoccupation with the written word, we sometimes overlook. Nobody, indeed, could well have had richer opportunities for hearing them than he—as a boy, from the lips of the denizens of Thames Street; from his fellow pages and Esquires at Court; from campaigners in Picardy; and from sailors and traffickers in merchandise throughout the long years in the Customs; from meetings by chance or design in the inns of London, and of Florence, Genoa, and Milan besides; and from his associates, drawn from every rank, condition, craft, and calling, in the multifarious occupations of his later years. 'Ye ben fadres of tydinges And tales', says the Man of Law, addressing merchants; and, he goes on:

I were right now of tales desolat,
Nere that *a marchaunt*, goon is many a yere,
Me taughte a tale, which that ye shal here.

Just this tale Chaucer read in a book; but the remark has no less point for that. And he knew whereof he spoke, too, when in the *House of Fame* he names shipmen and pilgrims and pardoners and couriers as tellers of tidings—and lies! When Chaucer brought together his nine and twenty in a company, picking them from classes every one of which he intimately knew, and set them telling tales, it was his own experience to which he lent the eternity of art.

But he also had abundant knowledge of tales and collections of tales in *books*. That he knew the *Decameron* there is no valid evidence. And even had he known it, his own originality would remain unimpugned. For Boccaccio's scheme is static, and his narrators all of a piece. There was, indeed, a contemporary Italian collection of *novelle* which has survived in a single abominably written manuscript, in which the stories are told on a pilgrimage, though all by a single member of the company. It is humanly possible that Chaucer, when in Italy, may have run across this collection of Sercambi's. But there is not the slightest evidence that he did, and the odds against it are overwhelming. And I am quite unable to see any reason for regarding Geoffrey Chaucer as incapable of turning to account, *sua sponte*, a general custom which he could not but have, times without number, observed, and in which he had probably taken part himself. Original genius sometimes does originate.

But other collections he certainly knew. And it cannot be kept too closely in mind, if we are to grasp the sheer genius of Chaucer's plan, that in these, as in most of the great collections, the stories are told either by one person only (as in Sercambi's peripatetic company), or else (as in the *Decameron*) by members of a stationary, relatively homogeneous group. Or else the collections exemplify some formula or other, and the stories run true to a predetermined type. Chaucer himself had made just such a collection in the *Legend of Good Women*—a sequence of tales confined to women, and to women, at that, with a specific difference: namely, faithfulness in love. And how it bored him before he dropped it, and with what unabashed candour he said so, we have already seen. In at least three other collections which he well knew the stories have a like common factor. In the *Legenda Aurea* they are all concerned with saints. In the *De Claris Mulieribus* Boccaccio, like Chaucer in the *Legend*, collected tales of women, their differentia this time being the possession of renown. In the *De Casibus* Boccaccio's subjects possess in common the calamitous experience of having fallen from their high estate. And Chaucer, in the person of the Monk, collected similar tragedies; and the Monk, before beginning, incautiously remarked that he had a hundred such tales in his cell; and Chaucer, through the combined protests of the Knight and Harry Bailly, unceremoniously and for ever cut him off at his seventeenth. It is fairly obvious that Chaucer, having tried them, was no longer drawn to collections of the static type.

Finally, his old friend John Gower brought together, in the *Confessio Amantis*, a huge collection of stories which did fall within a frame. But the frame was as rigid as a structural steel skeleton. For the tales were all told by one teller (namely Genius, the Priest of Love), to one listener (the Lover), to exemplify one theme—to wit, the Seven Deadly Sins, in all their endless twigs and branches. And they constitute the most mercilessly categorized and inflexible collection that I know.

And so, when Chaucer conceived the idea of his pilgrimage, with its leisured movement through the English countryside in spring, along the ancient and familiar Pilgrims' Way; with its heterogeneous company—lay and ecclesiastical, gentle and low-born, ribald and devout—drawn from half the ranks, professions, occupations, trades, and crafts that he had intimately known; when they talked and jested and argued and flared up in quarrels as they went; when the motley company of tellers told their tales in keeping with their kinds; and when an immortal innkeeper of Southwark exercised the offices of guide and autocrat and arbiter in one—when that plan was conceived in Chaucer's brain a new thing appeared under the sun.

VI. THE HUMAN COMEDY

I HAVE chosen to follow the unfolding of Chaucer's genius up to its crowning achievement in the *Canterbury Tales* instead of giving to them the lion's share. For to most of us the masterpiece is more familiar than the evolution of the powers which created it. And now I must pay for my choice. For summary measures are inescapable, when infinite riches must be crowded into the little room of a single hour.

I

There had never before, in the first place, been the like of that singularly *modern* thing—to use our most complacent term of approbation—the Prologue. Descriptions of individuals Chaucer knew by the gross. And at least one list of such descriptions, which after a fashion had served as a prologue, he certainly knew—that series of 'Portraits' of the heroes and heroines of the Trojan war, which Benoit inserts in the *Roman de Troie*. But in its essays at characterization Benoit's bead-roll stands to Chaucer's Prologue as a nursery-tale stands to the *Troilus*. Its thirty-two portraits follow in benumbing iteration a set formula, and except for Briseida's and Helen's eyebrows, and Nestor's hooked nose, and Neoptolemus's huge belly, and Priam's love for tales and songs, and Cassandra's power of divination, you might shuffle the names, and then shuffle the descriptive details, and, save for keeping men and women apart, put the list together again as chance decreed and never a soul in a thousand would be the wiser. 'Grove nods at grove, each Alley has a brother.' And such canonical descriptions, answering each other in noses, eyes, mouths, chins, and hair, occur by the score in the pages of twelfth-, thirteenth-, and fourteenth-century poetry. An *individual* among them is like 'the soleyn fenix of Arabye'.

Dante, to be sure, had broken the mould and etched and incised his graphic portraiture. Farinata degli Uberti, rising upright from his tomb in the Inferno, with breast and countenance as if he entertained great scorn of Hell; Sordello's solitary shade— 'O Lombard soul, how wast thou haughty and disdainful!'—watching with eyes grave and slow, after the fashion of a lion when he couches; Matilda, like Proserpine gathering flowers, and Beatrice, like the dawn; Ulysses, revealing in enthralling narrative *l'ardore . . . a divenir del mondo esperto*—these are figures seen thrown against their background as by a lightning flash. But the emergence of a character, step by step, through a succession of concrete details which fall in the end into perspective and reveal a person, *totus, teres, atque rotundus*—that, like the scheme of the Pilgrimage, was a new thing in the world. 'Anyman'—to apply the terse phrase of a recent editor of the *Characters* of Theophrastus—'Anyman has come to be Somebody'. And garb, and the manner of sitting a horse, and beards, and physiognomy merge with salient traits of personality to give a series of living portraits which, after five hundred years, remains unrivalled.

Those figures meet us for the first time in the Prologue. And at once we are faced by a question. Are they real persons—as Chaucer himself, or Langland, or Gower are real? Or are they purely Chaucer's creations—as Falstaff, or Hamlet, or Portia are Shakespeare's? Or are they both? The question has been lately raised in a brilliant and provocative volume, *Some New Light on Chaucer*, by one of the most distinguished of Chaucerian scholars, Professor Manly, who has argued, on the basis of newly gathered facts, that in several figures of the Prologue Chaucer did have definite persons in mind. There was, as has long been known, a Harry Bailly of Southwark who kept an inn, and thanks to recently discovered records we now know more. There are reasons, curious and tantalizing, which lead one to suspect that in the Reeve of Baldeswell Chaucer may have paid his respects to a rascally reeve whom he personally knew. And there were for the Man of Law, and the Franklin and Shipman besides, contemporary figures who offer more or less striking parallels. Were these figures, therefore, Chaucer's prototypes?

The facts do not warrant categorical statements, nor does Professor Manly make them. That there were here and there through the Prologue allusions which some of Chaucer's hearers would catch and savour there can be no doubt. But that is not to say that the portraits of the Prologue, as portraits, had living models to such a degree that contemporary listeners would exclaim when they heard them: 'That is the man!' Persons of every sort and condition represented in the Prologue had been intimately known to Chaucer through years crowded with experience and observation. What the portraits actually do, all conjecture aside, is to strike the delicate balance between the *character*, in the technical, Theophrastian sense of the word, and the *individual*—a balance which preserves at once the typical qualities of the one and the human idiosyncrasies of the other. Observation, in a word, has been caught up into the moulding energy of the creative act. Chaucer may well have had that piratical rogue John Hawley of Dartmouth in the back of his mind when he drew the Shipman. But if so, the Shipman assuredly has ceased to be John Hawley. He is the incarnation of the type to which John Hawley, and a score of his congeners, belonged. And one line alone—'With many a tempest hadde his berd been shake'—sets him, like the Flying Dutchman and the Ancient Mariner, among the immortals who in their spheres are every one and no one. I know no such illuminating commentary on the Prologue as Professor Manly's book; but the question of actual identifications must still, I think, be held *sub judice*.

But the Prologue is more than a prologue. It is an integral part of the plan as a whole. And that plan is unique in that the tales are part and parcel of a largely conceived and organically unified structure. The Prologue gives us the *tellers*—statically, in their potentialities. But as the cavalcade moves on the static becomes dynamic. Antagonisms flame up; a drunken pilgrim insists on telling his tale out of turn;

the Shipman flatly refuses to hear a sermon from the
Parson and promises a tale that will wake the company up; a cleric drinks too much corny ale and his
tongue is unclerically loosed; a boresome tale is cut
short and one thereby learns something new about
the distinguished interrupter; a lively discussion about
marriage springs up and tales, informative and lively,
are told in support of divergent views. The company,
in a word, that gathered in Southwark at the Tabard
were there in precisely the position of any shipload
of travellers as the ship leaves port. What follows has
its closest analogy in the smoking-room as the voyage
goes on. And in the links between the tales Chaucer
has made the most original of all his contributions.
The tales are not isolated entities. They stand in intimate relation to all that Chaucer in the Prologue has
revealed about their tellers, and also to the give and
take of dialogue which in the linking narrative leads
up to them and follows them. The *Canterbury Tales*,
even though their plan remains a splendid torso only,
are an organic whole, and that whole is essentially
dramatic. 'Dialogue and action, gesture, costume and
scenery, as in real life'—all are there. Long before
Balzac Chaucer conceived and exhibited the Human
Comedy.

And in the person of the Host he did something in
English letters startlingly new: he created his *Chorus*.
The Prologue gives us the pilgrims *in statu quo ante*;
their own actions along the road reveal their characters; but (to propound an axiom) it is only when you
see yourself as an inn-keeper or a butler sees you that

you know the whole truth about yourself. In either case, you are apt to be sadder as well as wiser. And Chaucer, with that art of his which shares with great creating nature, has shown us the pilgrims not only through his own and through each other's eyes but also through the eyes of Harry Bailly. Take the *Canterbury Tales* some day and read nothing but the remarks of that incomparable Boniface. The Eagle of the *House of Fame*, who would have adorned alike a professorial chair or the tap-room of an inn, after a long and acute and surprisingly correct demonstration of the way in which sound travels through the air, asked Chaucer if he has understood it. And Chaucer, shuddering, answered 'Yis'. 'A ha!' said the Eagle, 'lo, so I can [speke] Lewedly to a lewed man.' Even so Harry Bailly, with an astuteness ripened through long years of observation in a London inn, accommodates his words to the several pilgrims with unerring nicety:

'My lady Prioresse, by your leve,
So that I wiste I sholde yow nat greve,
I wolde demen that ye tellen sholde
A tale next, if so were that ye wolde.
Now wol ye vouche-sauf, my lady dere?'

So, again, with a courtesy this time touched with that benignant affability with which the man of the world indulges the scholar, the Host addresses the Clerk of Oxford:

'Sir clerk of Oxenford', our hoste sayde,
'Ye ryde as coy and stille as dooth a mayde . . .
This day ne herde I of your tonge a word.
I trow ye studie aboute som sophyme . . .

For goddes sake, as beth of bettre chere,
It is no tyme for to studien here.
Telle us som mery tale, by your fey.'

But—

'Sir monk, na-more of this, so god yow blesse!
Your tale anoyeth al this companye;
Swich talking is nat worth a boterflye . . .
For sikerly, nere clinking of your belles,
That on your brydel hange on every syde,
By heven king, that for us alle dyde,
I sholde er this han fallen doun for slepe.'

Read the words of the Host, which precipitate a double explosion, in the Prologue to the *Shipman's Tale*; read what he says, after hearing the sad story of Appius and Virginia, for the most engaging embodiment I know of the attitude of a typical audience at melodrama; and above all read his impassioned outburst in the Monk's Prologue on the monstrous regiment of Godelief his wife. For with the pilgrims, Chaucer declares and demonstrates, the Host spoke 'as lordly as a king'. But at home—*le roi est mort; vive la reine!* And never did browbeaten husband unpack his heart with more soul-satisfying words. The conception of the *Canterbury Tales* as drama is Chaucer's masterpiece.

The drama was still in its plastic state when Chaucer left it, and even the order in which he meant his groups of tales to stand remains in some instances in doubt. And he had also in mind certain shifts between tales and tellers which he never completely carried through. The most fiercely masculine of the Pilgrims, the Shipman, is made, *as teller*, to remark in his Tale, apropos of that pitiable thing, a husband:

> He moot *us* clothe, and he moot *us* arraye . . .
> In which array *we* daunce jolily.

That this feminine phraseology was not originally designed for that bearded and be-daggered buccaneer the Shipman is as obvious as that the Tale was first meant for the Wife of Bath. Then the Wife was given another Tale which faultlessly dovetails with her Prologue, and her first was transferred, for adjustment later, to the Shipman—who would, I am sure, have told it with no less gusto than the Wife herself. *Per contra*, the Second Nun, in the Prologue of her Tale, employs the words: 'I, unworthy *sone* of Eve'; and the Man of Law, remarking quite superfluously that he would be loath to be likened to the Muses, declares: 'I speke in *prose*'—while the Tale which he actually tells is in *verse*. But in essentials Chaucer's great conception stands secure. The drama of the pilgrimage, as Chaucer conceived it, is a greater achievement than any single Tale. But the Tales are at once the *raison d'être* of the drama and integral factors in its development. They are told, at their best, with consummate art—an art which in the end eludes analysis. Their craftsmanship, however, we may follow with modesty enough. And an obvious starting-point is their beginnings and their endings.

II

I know no way in which the singular effectiveness of Chaucer's openings, regarded as introductions,

may be more swiftly and compendiously shown than
by setting down a dozen of them in isolation from their
contexts, and without reference to their sequence in
the *Tales*. 'Lo here', then (to borrow Chaucer's
phrase) 'the forme':

Whylom ther was dwellinge at Oxenford
A riche gnof, that gestes heeld to bord,
And of his craft he was a Carpenter.
With him ther was dwellinge a povre scoler.

At Trumpington, nat fer fro Cantebrigge,
Ther goth a brook and over that a brigge,
Up-on the whiche brook ther stant a melle;
And this is verray soth that I yow telle.
A Miller was ther dwelling many a day;
As eny pecok he was proud and gay.

A Prentis whylom dwelled in our citee,
And of a craft of vitaillers was he;
Gaillard he was as goldfinch in the shawe,
Broun as a berie, a propre short felawe.

A Marchant whylom dwelled at Seint Denys,
That riche was, for which men helde him wys,
A wyf he hadde of excellent beautee,
And compaignable and revelous was she.

A povre widwe, somdel stape in age,
Was whylom dwelling in a narwe cotage,
Bisyde a grove, stonding in a dale . . .
Three large sowes hadde she, and namo,
Three kyn, and eek a sheep that highte Malle.

In Flaundres whylom was a companye
Of yonge folk, that haunteden folye,
As ryot, hasard, stewes, and tavernes,
Wher-as, with harpes, lutes, and giternes,
They daunce and pleye at dees bothe day and night.

In th' olde dayes of the King Arthour,
Of which that Britons speken greet honour,
Al was this land fulfild of fayerye.

When Phebus dwelled here in this erthe adoun,
As olde bokes maken mencioun,
He was the moste lusty bachiler
In al this world, and eek the beste archer.

At Sarray, in the land of Tartarye,
Ther dwelte a king, that werreyed Russye . . .
This noble king was cleped Cambinskan.

In Surrie whylom dwelte a companye
Of chapmen riche, and therto sadde and trewe,
That wyde-wher senten her spycerye,
Clothes of gold, and satins riche of hewe.

Whylom, as olde stories tellen us,
Ther was a duk that highte Theseus;
Of Athenes he was lord and governour . . .
That gretter was ther noon under the sonne.

In Armorik, that called is Britayne,
Ther was a knight that loved and dide his payne
To serve a lady in his beste wyse.

Without preamble or a wasted word the story is given
the ποῦ στῶ from which it is to spring. Chaucer is
using one of the oldest, most straightforward and
effective opening devices in the world. It is simply
a glorified 'Once upon a time'. And 'Once upon a
time', which is exactly Chaucer's 'whylom', not only
gives a fillip to the imagination but also leads straight
as an arrow into the tale. The formula has been used
by the tellers of tales since the days when stories began
to be told.

M

There was a king before now, and he married, and he had but one daughter. When his wife departed, he would marry none but one whom her clothes would fit.

There was ere now a poor old fisher, but on this year he was not getting much fish. On a day of days, and he fishing, there rose a sea-maiden at the side of his boat.

Vor Zeiten lebte eine alte Königin, die war eine Zauberin, und ihre Tochter war das schönste Mädchen unter der Sonne.

Es war einmal ein steinaltes Mütterchen, das lebte mit seiner Herde Gänse in einer Einöde zwischen Bergen und hatte da ein kleines Haus.

That is the unerring instinct of the folk-tale. The trick is neither literary nor academic; it is instinctive and universal.

I first brought together my array of Chaucerian openings, as it happened, while sitting in an inn—but not, alas! in Southwark at the Tabard. I walked upstairs when I had finished, and on a landing two old ladies sat in talk. As I passed I heard these words, which I set down as soon as I was round the corner: 'His mother was a widow, and had a little trimming store in Chester.' I missed the initial statement and do not know who 'he' was, or what was next to follow. But I remembered: 'A povre widwe, somdel stape in age, Was whylom dwelling in a narwe cotage'— five hundred years before. And when I reached my room, with that startling conjunction of immemorial and immediate in mind, I picked up the current number of our weekly surrogate for Canterbury Tales, *The Saturday Evening Post*, which I had just bought from

a miniature replica of Chaucer's Merchant in the
street. And the first story at which I opened began:

In that part of Boston that is known as the Fenway are
a great many furnished apartments, occupied by men with
white-collar jobs. . . . In the parlor of one of these apartments, upon a Spring evening, sat three men smoking.

Then I did what I should first have done. I opened
the Bible with which the Gideons had provided me,
and the first narrative passage to which I came, turning the leaves at random, began thus:

Now there was a certain man of Ramathaim-zophim,
of mount Ephraim, and his name was Elkanah, the son
of Jeroham . . . an Ephrathite. And he had two wives;
the name of the one was Hannah, and the name of the
other Peninnah: and Peninnah had children, but Hannah
had no children.

And so the great story of Samuel begins. And once
more, there you are! The stage is set; the *dramatis
personae* begin to appear; and the Aristotelian defini-
tion of a beginning has been fulfilled. The formula
is born, not made; before Abraham was, for that
matter, it was.

Chaucer, in a word, in using the familiar opening,
is practising the fine economy of art. And I, for
one, moreover, when the succinct initial sentences
lay in bird's-eye view before me, first fully grasped
the scope and variety of the background against which
the tales are thrown. Athens, Oxford, Cambridge,
London, Syria, France, Asia, the English country-
side, Flanders, Arthurian Britain, Yorkshire, Lombardy, Tartary, Brittany, the ancient world when

Phœbus Apollo dwelt with men, an alchemist's laboratory in London—the range of Chaucer's settings is scarcely less extraordinary than the rich diversity of the figures who are thrown against them.

The *endings* of the tales, too, are only less suggestive than their openings. For the stories are told by pilgrims, and the pilgrims all dimly felt, or perforce acknowledged, what the Parson alone, in his prologue, put into words:

> And Jesu, for his grace, wit me sende
> To shewe yow the wey, in this viage,
> Of *thilke parfit glorious pilgrimage*
> That highte Jerusalem celestial.

And so all the tales but half a dozen close with a prayer, or a pious injunction.

> Thus endeth Palamon and Emelye;
> And God save al this faire companye!—Amen.

So ends the Knight his tale.

> This tale is doon, and god save al the route!

That is the Miller's line at the end of a ribald summary; and the respective qualities of knight and churl are as patent in their closing lines as in their narratives. Not even a prayer can keep the Reeve's malicious triumph in his *quid pro quo* to the Miller from breaking out:

> And God, that sitteth heighe in magestee,
> Save al this companye grete and smale!
> *Thus have I quit the miller in my tale.*

The Friar, who has just made it clear beyond peradventure where Somnours go when they die, blends in his epilogue venom and piety:

But, for to kepe us fro that cursed place,
Waketh, and preyeth Jesu for his grace
So kepe us fro the temptour Sathanas . . .
And prayeth that thise Somnours hem repente
Of hir misdedes, er that the feend hem hente.

And the Wife of Bath remains irrepressible:

And thus they live, un-to hir lyves ende,
In parfit joye; and Jesu Crist us sende
Housbondes meke, yonge, and fresshe abedde,
And grace t'overbyde hem that we wedde.
And eek I preye Jesu shorte hir lyves
That wol nat be governed by hir wyves;
And olde and angry nigardes of dispence,
God sende hem sone verray pestilence.

The tales are knit up through their endings with the pilgrimage. And in yet another fashion, unobtrusively but with considered art, the structural elements of Chaucer's plan are bound together as by filaments of steel.

III

Now Chaucer invented none of his tales. But they came to him, broadly speaking, in two different ways —through books and through oral tradition. And his freedom in the handling of his narratives is determined, both in kind and in degree, by the medium through which his stories reached him. The tales of the Knight, the Man of Law, of Chaucer himself in *Melibeus*, of the Monk, the Physician, the Clerk, the Second Nun, and in less degree those of the Prioress and the Manciple, are taken over, with varying directness, from *books*. Chaucer's treatment of them, nevertheless, is all his own, and to follow what he does with what he finds is to gain illuminating insight into both his art and his originality. In the *Knight's Tale*, to take but one instance, he reverses his procedure in the *Troilus*. There, through his absorption in a deeply human problem, he expanded Boccaccio's *Filostrato* to half its length again. In the *Knight's Tale*, on the contrary, he reduces Boccaccio's narrative in the *Teseide* to a fourth of its original length, and three-fourths of what he actually tells has no parallel in his original. And Emelye, in startling contrast with Criseyde, speaks but twice in all the poem. Both narratives, *Troilus* and *Knight's Tale*—which stand to each other almost as *Hamlet* stands to *Henry V*—are, as Chaucer tells them, free rehandlings of their originals, but they are independent in utterly different ways, and both ways are characteristic of Chaucer. And the other tales in the group are told—for the teller was Chaucer—with a freedom now greater, now less.

But it is not in the tales which he draws directly from books that Chaucer himself, man and artist, most characteristically appears. For that we must go to the tales which came down to him, in varying degrees of directness, through long tradition—tales, it may be, which had lived on men's lips for centuries, passing current in every tongue, and worn down to their bare nucleus. And that kernel was commonly an incident or a situation, protean in its potentialities, and changing from land to land and century to century its setting through its wanderings. And the tales which have such ancestry, and which so offered Chaucer untrammelled opportunities for their development, are—in varying fashions and degrees—the tales of the Miller, Reeve, Shipman, Nun's Priest, Pardoner, Wife of Bath, Somnour, Friar, Merchant, and Squire. These are the tales in which Chaucer is most supremely Chaucer. The very baldness of the central situation liberates him to create his own characters and setting, and it is in these stories that his individual genius has freest play to run and be glorified. It is, then, upon those tales which in a peculiar sense are Chaucer's own that I shall chiefly draw. The great figures of the Prioress, and Constance, and Griselda, and the 'litel clergeon', and Arveragus and Dorigen, and St. Cecilia—pure, lovely, and of good report—have already had their meed of praise a hundred times.

Five of the traditional tales, it must be said at once, deal with situations, not of Chaucer's making, which are frankly scurrilous or indecent. They belong to a time less squeamish than ours, but even so, Chaucer entered a caveat:

> And ther-fore every gentil wight I preye,
> For goddes love, demeth nat that I seye
> Of evel entente, but that I moot reherce
> Hir tales alle, be they bettre or werse,
> Or elles falsen som of my matere.
> And therfore, who-so list it nat y-here,
> Turne over the leef, and chese another tale . . .
> Blameth nat me if that ye chese amis.

And for many these tales are marred by their breach of decorum. The Miller's, Reeve's, Somnour's, and

Merchant's tales and the Wife of Bath's Prologue, with their occasional frank unseemliness, are not milk for babes. But in Chaucer's hands bald and vulgar incidents which had gone to and fro on the earth for centuries evoked, after the singular ways of genius, masterpieces of characterization. For he never surpassed, I think, the art displayed in a few of these tales. The Miller's and Reeve's tales, save in their endings, together with the Friar in the *Somnour's Tale*, the Wife of Bath, the Pardoner, Harry Bailly, and Madame Pertelote are perhaps Chaucer's greatest creations in the *Canterbury Tales*. And all save Madame Pertelote are, I fear, more or less engaging rascals. But that mystery I leave, as Chaucer left predestination, 'to divynis', and return to the safe and quiet harbour of technique.

In most of these tales, then, which are peculiarly his, Chaucer instead of plunging *in medias res*, brings on the stage at once his *dramatis personae*. And his descriptions of them rival and sometimes surpass the portraits of the Prologue. Three of the most vivid are those of the two conspirators and one of the dupes in the *Miller's Tale*—'hende Nicholas', Alisoun (the Miller's fair and frail young wife), and Absolon, the parish clerk. And the three are described with a brilliance and abandon which the more staid depictions in the Prologue rarely attain. Nicholas, who is a Clerk of Oxford, is drawn with the Clerk of the Prologue palpably in mind, and his portrait is an ironical variation upon the earlier theme. And the portrayal of Alisoun is a masterpiece. Except in the account of the Prioress, I know no passage which more signally displays Chaucer's power of pouring new life into hackneyed moulds. The portrait runs faultlessly true in its method to the stock conventions for depicting feminine beauty—those conventions which, with devastating uniformity, list the lady's charms in scores upon scores of fourteenth-century and earlier French poems. Forehead, eyes, nose, mouth, chin, throat, and on without let or hindrance —the lady is anatomized in good set similes as inescapable as death. Chaucer has kept the mould and thrown to the winds the stock details that fill it. And he has gone for his similes not to the books but straight to the English country-side.

> Fair was this yonge wyf, and ther-with-al
> *As any wesele* hir body gent and smal.

Her apron was '*as whyt as morne milk*'; her brows as '*blake as any sloo*':

> She was ful more blisful on to see
> Than is the *newe pere-jonette tree;*
> And softer than *the wolle is of a wether*. . .
> But of hir song, it was as loude and yerne
> As any *swalwe sittinge on a berne* . . .
> Hir mouth was swete as *bragot or the meeth,*
> Or *hord of apples leyd in hey or heeth.*
> Winsinge she was, *as is a joly colt,*
> Long as a mast, and upright as a bolt.

But for one detail Chaucer returns, in a fleeting glimpse, to the scenes of his own official life:

> Ful brighter was the shyning of hir hewe
> Than *in the tour* the noble y-forged newe.

With a relish which one feels in every line, he has vivified the dead conventions and set them playing truant in the fields, and even in the Tower—the Tower where he as a little page had gone to see the lions, and from which, in less glamorous years, he had to account for a frying-pan.

And in Absolon, who when not about the parish business was a barber, Chaucer gives, with unerring touches, the portrait of a typical small-town dandy. I have seen him, you have seen him; for barring the accidents of costume, he still walks the streets of any country town. He is an eternal type made individual through a local habitation and a name. And with uncanny accuracy Chaucer gives first of all the trick which most infallibly marks the rustic beau—the fearsome fashion in which he combs his hair. And Absolon, being a barber, was *au fait* in the latest masculine coiffure. And his shoes, too, are *à la mode*, with a window of St. Paul's engagingly carved in the leather; and he has on red hose and a light blue kirtle, and (being parish clerk as well as barber) wears over the kirtle a gay surplice, white as the blossom on the spray. And his *savoir faire* was no less manifest in his dancing:

> In twenty manere coude he trippe and daunce
> *After the scole of Oxenforde tho*,
> And with his legges casten to and fro.

And when, no longer a barber but a parish clerk, he swung the censer on holy-days, he waved the incense with love-lorn glances towards the ladies of the parish, and especially towards the Carpenter's pretty wife:

To loke on hir him thoughte a mery lyf,
She was so propre and swete and likerous.
I dar wel seyn, if she had been a mous,
And he a cat, he wolde hir hent anon.

The thing again is a masterpiece, in which Chaucer
has delightedly let himself go. And seldom with
swifter and surer touches has a type been made
incarnate in an individual.

In the *Reeve's Tale*, too, three of the five characters
are brought at once upon the stage and drawn with
no less swift and telling strokes—the Miller, 'dëynous
Simkin', moon-faced, flat-nosed, bald as an ape, a
touchy swaggerer, ready for anybody, with a small
arsenal of weapons on his person—in his belt 'a long
panade', 'a joly popper' in his pouch, and a 'Sheffeld
thwitel' in his hose. His wife, says Chaucer, was of
noble kin: 'The person of the toun hir fader was'. And
that laconic statement veils for us an irony which to
the Pilgrims carried instant comprehension. For
parsons then were celibates. And so she had been
fostered not at home, for she had none, but in a nun-
nery. And a subtle reading of human nature under-
lies the next detail. For 'she was proud, and pert as
is a pye', and stand-offish, and contemptuous: her
instinctive, defensive reaction to the stigma of her
birth. But—if anybody called her anything but
'Madame', Simkin (another infallible touch) was
ready with his arsenal. And it was a 'ful fair sighte',
says Chaucer, to see them bound for church on holy-
days—he before her, with his tipet wound about his
head, while she came after in a gown of red, 'and

Simkin hadde hosen of the same'. And they had one
daughter, a plump wench, with her father's nose. It
is, in a word, a *family* this time, which Chaucer has
drawn with the sureness of touch that marks his
maturest art. Then into the life of the trio come two
care-free and irresponsible young clerks of Cambridge. And them we learn to know through the
matching of their wits against the Miller's, talking
the while in good north country dialect, as the brilliant
narrative proceeds to its unseemly end.

What, now—passing from Chaucer's technique in
bringing his characters on the stage, and still drawing
upon the group which is peculiarly his own—what
may be said of the *settings* of the tales?

Chaucer's craftsmanship in those tales in which he
worked with a free hand is unsurpassed, I think, in
English poetry. And for pure virtuosity the *Miller's
Tale*, in which setting and action are interwoven as
in a close-knit texture, is perhaps his masterpiece.
The scene of the story is laid in Oxford, and the
references to Osenay establish Chaucer's intimate
knowledge of the topography of the town. But the
specific *setting* of the tale is the carpenter's house,
never described, but building itself up by degrees
before us, as detail after detail prints itself on the eye
—the shot-window in the wall; the gable facing the
garden and the stable; the garret under the roof, with
its transverse beams; the hole in a board of the wall
through which the cat used to creep—Vermeer or
Ostade could have painted it on Chaucer's hints. And
the tale is pervaded by foreshadowings and sugges-

tions which create that intangible thing which we call atmosphere. About the four halves of the house and on the threshold of the outer door the duped and doltish carpenter, making the sign of the cross, utters the night-spell to ward off (the mocking irony is consummate) elves and wights:

'Jesu Crist, and sëynt Benedight,
Blesse this hous from every wikked wight,
For nightes verye, the white *paternoster*!—
Where wentestow, seynt Petres soster?'

And like an ominous chorus to the action, echoes of the miracle-plays keep pace with the tale. Absolon, to display his lightness and dexterity, had played Herod 'on a scaffold hye'. And the anguish which Noah suffered before he could get his wife into the ark is invoked by Nicholas, to sinister ends, in further-ance of his graceless plot. In none of the other tales is the weave of the piece so close and firm.

The setting of the *Reeve's Tale*, drawn like that of the Miller's from personal knowledge, and like it steeped in local colour, is sketched with broader strokes—except for the final touch of the hole in the chamber-wall, through which this time no cat was wont to creep, but into which, with a little shimmer-ing of light, the moon shone to precipitate the *dénoue-ment*. And these two tales must serve, for the realistic group, as examples of Chaucer's craftsmanship in the setting of his tales.

In the *Wife of Bath's Tale* and the *Squire's Tale* Chaucer passes for his background into another world, the world of *Faërye*, or enchantment. The Wife of

Bath, as she begins her tale, looks back in lines of
perennial charm to the days of that 'unsubstantial
faery' world that was gone. And again one marvels
at the closeness with which Chaucer's fabric, as a
complex whole, is knit. For the Wife's diagnosis of
the occasion of its passing binds up her tale with the
quarrel between the Somnour and the Friar which
has just interrupted her flow. The Somnour has burst
out: 'Lo!... goddes armes two! A frere wol entre-
mette him ever-mo. Lo, gode men, a flye and eek
a frere Wol falle in every dish and eek matere.'
Friars, in a word, thrust themselves into everything,
and spoil it. And as the Wife begins her Tale, with
a woman's quick wit she turns the quarrel to her
purpose:

> In th' olde dayes of the king Arthour,
> Of which that Britons speken greet honour,
> Al was this land fulfild of fayerye.
> The elf-queen, with hir joly companye,
> Daunced ful ofte in many a grene mede...
> But now can no man see none elves mo.
> *For now the grete charitee and prayeres*
> *Of limitours and othere holy freres ...*
> *This maketh that there been no fayeryes.*
> For ther as wont to walken was an elf,
> Ther walketh now the limitour himself.

The world is too small for both friars and fairies!
And the story itself, which is as old as the Celtic hills,
is told with a felicity and clothed with a beauty which
it had never attained before.

In the *Squire's Tale*, too, it is magic and illusion
and enchanted princesses, in that remote and mys-

terious Orient where anything may happen, which form the background of the half-told tale which so captivated Milton. The strange knight who rides into the hall on the steed of brass, with the magic mirror in his hand, and on his thumb the magic ring, and by his side the magic sword, spoke with 'so heigh reverence and obeisaunce',

> That Gawain, with his olde curteisye,
> Though he were come ageyn *out of Fairye*,
> Ne coude him nat amende with a word.

And when the throng gathered about the horse of brass,

> . . . evermore hir moste wonder was,
> How that it coude goon, and was of bras;
> *It was of Fairye*, as the peple semed.

It is the glamour of that world which Chaucer, turning for a moment from his world of wool and hides and ditches, and Millers and Monks and Manciples, sheds upon these two tales.

Faërye, which lends an elfish humour to Sir Thopas, appears for a moment, too, in the sordid course of the *Merchant's Tale*, but now it is Pluto and Proserpine who rule its realm. For January, who had married May ('Hir to biholde it semed *fayërye*'),

> [Had] made a gardin, walled al with stoon;
> So fair a gardin woot I nowher noon.
> For out of doute, I verraily suppose,
> That he that wroot the Romance of the Rose
> Ne coude of it the beautee wel devyse;
> Ne Priapus ne mighte nat suffyse,
> Though he be god of gardins, for to telle
> The beautee of the gardin and the welle,

That stood under a laurer alwey grene.
Ful ofte tyme he, Pluto, and his quene,
Proserpina, and *al hir fayërye*
Disporten hem and maken melodye
Aboute that welle, and daunced, as men tolde.

Then, as the gross *dénouement* of the tale approaches,

[It] so bifel, that brighte morwe-tyde,
That in that gardin, in the ferther syde,
Pluto, *that is the king of fayërye*,
And many a lady in his companye,
Folwinge his wyf, the quene Proserpyne,
Ech after other, right as any lyne—
Whyl that she gadered floures in the mede,
In Claudian ye may the story rede,
How in his grisly carte he hir fette:—
This king of fairye thanne adoun him sette
Up-on a bench of turves, fresh and grene.

And thereupon Pluto and Proserpine—like the chorus
in Greek tragedy, or the gallants on the Elizabethan
stage—indulge in a brisk and racy domestic difference
over the masculine attitude towards women, in which,
with a point-blank bluntness worthy of the Wife of
Bath, Proserpine secures the upper hand. And with
enchanting anachronism the pair invoke 'this Jew, this
Salomon', and other scriptural worthies—the timeless denizens of Faërye having no more need than
the romancers to vex their heads about chronology.
Chaucer knew, for he elsewhere quotes the great
canto, Dante's lovely reference to Proserpina in his
words to Matilda gathering flowers in the Garden of
the *Purgatorio*. But this militant defender of her sex
is not Dante's Proserpina. Chaucer's art, in the epi-

sode, is subdued to what it works in, like the dyer's hand. The pall of the most cynically disillusioned of all the Tales has fallen on the enchanted landscape, and Faërye itself is tarnished.

It is saved as by fire, even there, through the beauty of its setting in the garden—a garden which is almost the replica of Chaucer's own, with its bench of turves, as he describes it in the Prologue to the *Legend*. But here it is linked besides with the garden and the welling spring beneath the evergreen, of which Guillaume de Lorris dreamed in the *Roman de la Rose*. And it is walled, with a little locked wicket in the wall, and it has pleasant alleys, like Criseyde's garden in the *Troilus*. It is, indeed, one of those walled and sequestered gardens which still come first to memory when one who knows them thinks of England. And whether Chaucer's scene be laid in the Troy of the romances, or not far from Pavia, or in Kent; and whether it be Criseyde and Antigone, or Pluto and Proserpine, or Chaucer himself, who walk in them, the setting for the moment becomes England, and five centuries are as a day.

IV

But Chaucer's ultimate glory is not his finished craftsmanship but the power by virtue of which he creates, through speech and action, living characters. Of his secret, as of God's—to paraphrase the drunken sapience of the Miller—it is unwise to be too inquisitive. 'Goddes foyson' is there in his accomplishment, and it is enough to dwell on that.

N

The greatest of Chaucer's portraits within the body of a tale is the Friar in the *Somnour's Tale*, as described in the first 250 lines or so of the narrative. I doubt if, within its compass, it has its match in English. But regarding the pilgrimage as a whole, Chaucer's masterpieces of characterization are, beyond question, the Pardoner and the Wife of Bath. Both lay bare their very selves with utter abandon—the Pardoner in a cynical disclosure, pitiless in its realism and daringly outspoken, of the hypocrisy of his preaching; the Wife of Bath (as a-moral as Falstaff and Rabelaisian before Rabelais) letting herself go with incomparable gusto and a frankness naked and unashamed, in an unexpurgated disclosure of her views upon marriage, and of her own successive marital adventures.

The Pardoner is evil to the core—the one lost soul, as Professor Kittredge once called him, among the pilgrims—with a single sharp moment of revulsion. And the tale which he tells is set as an *exemplum* in a sermon on avarice, with *radix malorum est cupiditas* as its text—a sermon rehearsed with flagrant cynicism as a taste of his quality. The tale, which is one of the world's oldest and most dramatic stories of greed and death, begins, is broken in upon by the savage intensity of the sermon, then sweeps to its close with perhaps the most haunting of all personifications of Death. Then, after his instant of self-realization, the Pardoner offers, with brazen disregard of his confession, his self-discredited pardons for sale, and his callously blown-upon relics to kiss, and with crown-

ing impudence singles out the host. And that precipi-
tates the tensest and most repugnant moment of the
journey. The whole is fearless and unsparing satire,
and prologue, tale, and setting together are dramatic
beyond any other unit of the Pilgrimage.

But it is the Wife of Bath who, as a figure, is the
greatest of them all. In every line of her Prologue
and in the whole, one feels Chaucer's sheer delight in
her creation. She is poured out, as it were, 'mit einem
Gusse'; she is absolutely of a piece. There is nothing
else quite like her. And her superb self-revelation,
with its verve and its raciness and its serenely ceaseless
flow, no more to be stopped (as the Pardoner found)
than the course of a planet; and above all (if Matthew
Arnold's austere shade will let me apply to her the
phrase which he applied to Goethe), her 'profound,
imperturbable naturalism'—all that is one of the few
achievements which actually create a personality.
John Galsworthy recently remarked, in speaking of
the dramatist's tendency to fashion types instead of
creating individuals: 'Falstaff is perhaps the greatest
exception to this rule. We think of the gorgeous old
ruffian first and last as a private person, without attach-
ing to him any particular phase of human character.'
And he and that other gorgeous old sinner, the Wife
of Bath, are in that respect two of a kind. They are
not types; they are persons.

Even the Wife's speech has its unanalysable,
individual, personal movement and turn. Wholly
apart from subject-matter, you could not mistake a
passage from the Pardoner's Prologue (for example)

for one of hers. Every human being who possesses anything approaching personality has his own unique rhythms, tones, inflexions, build of sentences. I have a friend, a distinguished man of letters, whose expression is so individual that a single line on a postcard will unconsciously and infallibly betray his authorship. And the Eagle, Pandare, and the Wife of Bath speak like themselves and like no one else. Chaucer, who wrote for the ear, heard (I think) as he wrote, every line he put into the mouth of his characters; and of these the most individual express that unique personal quality which marks them, in the idiosyncrasies, the idiom, the very movement of their speech. Wholly apart from the sense of the words, nobody but the Wife of Bath could have uttered these lines:

> Thou seydest this, that I was lyk a cat;
> For who-so wolde senge a cattes skin,
> Thanne wolde the cat wel dwellen in his in;
> And if the cattes skin be slyk and gay,
> She wol nat dwelle in house half a day,
> But forth she wole, er any day be dawed,
> To shewe hir skin, and goon a-caterwawed;
> This is to seye, if I be gay, sir shrewe,
> I wol renne out, my borel for to shewe.

Or this:

> Now wol I tellen of my fourthe housbonde . . .
> By god, in erthe I was his purgatorie,
> For which I hope his soule be in glorie . . .
> He deyde whan I cam fro Jerusalem,
> And lyth y-grave under the rode-beem . . .
> *It nis but wast to burie him preciously* . . .
> Yet was I never with-outen purveyance

Of mariạge, n'of othere thinges eek.
I holde a mouses herte nat worth a leek,
That hath but oon hole for to sterte to,
And if that faille, thanne is al y-do.

Or, above all, this:

But, lord Crist! whan that it remembreth me
Up-on my yowthe, and on my jolitee,
It tikleth me aboute myn herte rote.
Unto this day it dooth myn herte bote
That I have had my world as in my tyme.

The Wife of Bath was close kin to Geoffrey Chaucer.
And if those last lines are not Chaucer himself to the
core, then I have read the *House of Fame*, and the
Troilus, and the greater *Tales* amiss.

And Chaucer understood her no less when he put
into her mouth a cry which sums up half the passion
and pain of the world:

Allas! allas! that ever love was sinne!

Nor is it out of keeping when, in the Wife's own tale
of Faërye which in its ending fits her Prologue like
a glove, the old hag who is a lovely lady in disguise
gives an exposition of *gentilesse* which sums up the
noblest thinking of the Middle Ages upon gentle
breeding and true courtesy. For the Wife of Bath had
a mind as keen as a sword-blade, and could rise to the
height of a great argument in the dramatic realization
of the lofty conception which lay at the heart of her
tale. Even we occasionally have great moments.

And that lofty discourse on *gentilesse*, which owes
much to Boethius and Jean de Meun, and which is
steeped in Dante, raises another question. I spoke

earlier of the shift of emphasis which came about
between books and life, as Chaucer passed, by way
of the *Troilus*, from the earlier poems to the *Canterbury Tales*—a shift whereby books passed from foreground to background, until life, rather than letters,
held the stage. That is true. But half our sense of
richness, as we read the tales, arises, whether we know
it or not, from the fact that they are still saturated
with the vitality and colour of Chaucer's reading. The
Wife of Bath herself is not less but more Chaucer's
because her speech is shot through with reminiscences
of Jean de Meun and St. Jerome and Eustache Deschamps and more besides. But the elements have been
distilled in Chaucer's alembic, and the result is something dreamed of by none of them—certainly not by
St. Jerome!—something indefeasibly and uniquely
Chaucer's own. The Wife's Prologue is not an epi-
phyte, but an oak, and the sap in its veins is drawn
from soil enriched by the tillage of centuries.

That plausible scoundrel, the Friar in the *Somnour's
Tale*, is paying his respects to the Somnour. And
Chaucer again remembered Jerome's words from his
diatribe against that *bête noire* of his, Jovinian: *Et tu,
ille formosus monachus, crassus, nitidus, dealbatus, et
quasi sponsus semper incedens*—'And thou, lovely
monk, fat, shiny, bepowdered, stepping like a bride-
groom.' In the Friar's mouth Jerome's taunt takes
on the Friar's coloration:

> Me thinketh they ben lyk Jovinian,
> *Fat as a whale, and walkinge as a swan;*
> *Al vinolent as botel in the spence.*

And as the passage proceeds it outdoes even St. Jerome
in robustness. The exquisite humour of Madame
Pertelote's diagnosis and remedies is the distillation
of Chaucer's wide reading in the medical treatises of
his day—a reading which enlivens other passages.
The *Franklin's Tale* is enriched from his knowledge
of natural magic, and the *Canon's Yeoman's Tale* from
his conversance with alchemical treatises, and the *Wife
of Bath's Tale* from his absorption in Dante's great
discourse on *nobiltà* in the *Convivio*. And constantly,
as he writes, his memory flashes back and forth among
his books, and his recollections, with colours caught
from their sojourn in his mind, are woven into the
texture of the tales. Scholars have sedulously gathered
them up and listed them, and the lists *per se* are as
dead and as dessicated as herbariums. In their context they are alive. For the *zest* of Chaucer's reading
communicates itself to his recollections, and his learning is permeated with his authentic personal quality.
And in different moods different tracts of his reading
come back to memory. When he is deeply moved
he is apt to remember Dante, and particularly that
passage in which Dante, too, was most profoundly
stirred—the sublime prayer of St. Bernard to Mary
with which the last canto of the *Paradiso* opens. It
is with one of Dante's majestic invocations that the
Troilus closes, and, blended with reminiscences of
the Bible and of the great hymns from the Service
of the Church, St. Bernard's prayer again lends grave
beauty to the Prologues of the Prioress and the
Second Nun. Or, *per contra*, some staid and erudite

passage will be touched with mischievous humour,
as if it had been dipped in some impish wizard's con-
verting spring—as when Chauntecleer gravely trans-
lates for Madame Pertelote a scrap of monkish Latin
which in *Melibeus* Chaucer had rendered with perfect
propriety:

> For, also siker as *In principio*,
> *Mulier est hominis confusio*;
> Madame, the sentence of this Latin is—
> Womman is mannes joye and al his blis.

Learning could not live long in Chaucer's mind
without assimilation to the temper of that bright
spirit.

And the reason, at least in part, is not far to seek.
Professor Garrod, who has the trick of setting down
penetrating critical judgements with the engaging
air of making casual remarks, once said of Matthew
Arnold: 'He thinks too much of the uses of literature,
and too little of its pleasures. He attaches too much
importance to taste, and too little to *relish*.' That last
is one of the reasons why Matthew Arnold never
really understood Chaucer. For I can think of no
other poet—Shakespeare being always *hors concours*
—who brought to both books and life such relish and
whose work is so instinct with zest. Some of the old
voyagers had it, and Dampier's description of *hoc-shu*,
and Oviedo's of the coco-nut, have a gusto not unworthy of Chaucer. Even he, I think, never surpassed in its kind his initial description of the Canon's
Yeoman, as by hard riding he overtakes the pilgrims
at Boghton under Blee. For never elsewhere has a

hot and sweating human being been metamorphosed
with such delectation into a masterpiece.

> His hakeney, that was al pomely grys,
> So swatte, that it wonder was to see . . .
> The hors eek that his yeman rood upon
> So swatte, that unnethe mighte it gon.
> Aboute the peytrel stood the foom ful hye,
> He was of fome al flekked as a pye . . .
> A clote-leef he hadde under his hood
> For swoot, and for to kepe his heed from hete.
> *But it was joye for to seen him swete!*
> His forheed dropped as a stillatorie.

If ever the Terentian *nihil humanum* was exempli-
fied, it is there! The Canon's Yeoman sweat magni-
ficently, gloriously; it was like looking on one of
Nature's wonders to observe him. And Chaucer's
individual, peculiar quality lies in large measure in
that eager appetence of his for life, to which nothing
was common or unclean. One meets it everywhere.
The Wife of Bath is talking about her gay gowns
which she wore (especially when her fourth husband
was safely away in London) to vigils and processions
and preachings and plays and marriages. Then, she
says,

> [I] wered upon my gaye scarlet gytes.
> *Thise wormes, ne thise motthes, ne thise mytes,*
> Upon my peril, frete hem never a deel.

The relish in that twice repeated 'thise', with its in-
effable familiarity, is beyond words. 'Worms, moths,
and mites' are simply worms, moths, and mites—only
that, and nothing more. '*Thise* wormes, *thise* motthes,
thise mytes' have become intimates—brothers and

sisters, like (with a difference!) St. Francis's 'our brother, the wind, and our sister water'. And the same graphic immediacy of conception in another passage vividly anthropomorphizes God. Prayers, says that affable arch-hypocrite the Somnour's Friar,

> prayeres
> Of charitable and chaste bisy freres
> Maken hir sours [flight] to *goddes eres two.*

The *ear* of God is little more than an abstraction —'Neither [is] his ear heavy, that it cannot hear.' 'God's *two ears*' startlingly visualizes, humanizes God. And the daring familiarity which the Friar allows himself is not only an apt touch in a masterpiece of satirical portraiture but also, once more, an instance of Chaucer's imaginative coalescence with his subject.

Moreover, every passage which, for other ends, I have quoted in this section brings sharply before us a kindred quality of Chaucer's mind—his instinct for the concrete. 'Thou seydest this, that I was lyk a cat'; 'I holde a mouses herte nat worth a leek, That hath but oon hole for to sterte to'; 'It tikleth me aboute myn herte rote'; 'Fat as a whale . . . walkinge as a swan . . . vinolent as botel in the spence'; 'Siker as *In principio*'; a sweating dapple-gray horse flecked with foam like a magpie; a burdock-leaf under a hood; a forehead dropping sweat like a still; worms, moths, and mites, and festive scarlet gowns; God's two ears. 'You poets', Landor makes Porson say in one of the *Imaginary Conversations*—'you poets are still rather too fond of the unsubstantial. Some will have nothing else than what they call pure imagination.... *I hate both poetry and wine without body.*' On that score Chaucer's withers are triumphantly unwrung! In a master's hand and in its place the concrete carries straight and true to the mark, as Dante, Villon, Bunyan, Defoe all knew, and none better than the writers of the great Biblical narratives. Turn to the stories of Jacob, or Joseph, or Moses, or Deborah, or to the closing chapters of the Book of Job, or the accounts of the betrayal in the garden, or the Revelation of St. John, and see what their vividness owes to concrete detail. Or re-read *Les regrets de la belle Heaulmière*, or *The Pilgrim's Progress*, or *Robinson Crusoe*. Then come back, for a new sense of their mastery, to the great tales in which Chaucer has a free hand.

Here, for example, are the lines in which the Reeve unexpectedly unlocks his heart:

Yet in our asshen olde is fyr y-reke . . .
Our olde lemes mowe wel been unwelde,
But wil ne shal nat faillen, that is sooth.
And yet ik have alwey a coltes tooth,
As many a yeer as it is passed henne
Sin that my tappe of lyf bigan to renne.
For sikerly, whan I was bore, anon
Deeth drogh the tappe of lyf and leet it gon;
And ever sith hath so the tappe y-ronne,
Til that almost al empty is the tonne.
The streem of lyf now droppeth on the chimbe.

And here, in the Pardoner's exposure of his homiletic tricks, is a picture so telling in its concrete realization of bodily action that one not only visualizes the movements but feels one's self incipiently reproducing them:

> Than peyne I me to strecche forth the nekke,
> And est and west upon the peple I bekke,
> *As doth a dowve sitting on a berne.*
> Myn hondes and my tonge goon so yerne,
> That it is joye to see my bisinesse—

as it was joy to see the Canon's Yeoman sweat! Relish and the concreteness which Landor called 'body' in Chaucer go hand in hand.

For as Milton's archangel's sky-tinctured wings were of colours dipt in heaven, the great Tales, as Chaucer tells them, are not merely dipt, but drenched, in life. And characters which came to him lay figures became in speech and action more vividly alive than most of us. Even a cock and hen, which he had found plain cock and hen, have become, without for a moment ceasing to be fowls, vivaciously and captivatingly human. Read the story of the *Nun's Priest's Tale* in any older version—beast fable or beast epic as you will—and see what Chaucer has done. And then, to see what Chaucer alone can do, read line by line with it the retelling of the tale by even so great a poet and master of the vernacular as Dryden.

> Pekke hem up right as they growe, and ete hem in.
> Be mery, housbond, for your fader kin!

That is Chaucer. Now John Dryden:

> Eat these, and be, my lord, of better cheer;
> Your father's son was never born to fear.

Or Chaucer again:

> Madame Pertelote, my worldes blis,

Herkneth thise blisful briddes how they singe,
And see the fresshe floures how they springe.

Then Dryden once more:

Then turning, said to Partlet: 'See, my dear,
How lavish nature has adorn'd the year;
How the pale primrose and blue violet spring,
And birds essay their throats disus'd to sing.

Whatever Chaucer touched, when what Byron called the *estro* was upon him, has a zest, a spontaneity, a raciness, which are inimitable and unique. The specific difference of the *Canterbury Tales* is their immersion in *life*—which is tantamount to saying (to amend my metaphor) that they are dipt in Geoffrey Chaucer.

Mutatis mutandis, that is true of his verse. And again I have the masterpieces especially in mind. For verse which retains the qualities of living speech—its turns, inflexions, stresses, *nuances*, which are its body, as we may call the incorporated sense its soul— such verse Chaucer wrote as few have ever written it. Here are three stanzas only of the swift, light touch-and-go of the dialogue between Pandare and Criseyde as the Second Book of the *Troilus* begins:

'As ever thryve I', quod this Pandarus,
'Yet coude I telle a thing to doon you pleye.'
'Now uncle dere,' quod she, 'tel it us
For goddes love; is than th' assege aweye?
I am of Grekes so ferd that I deye.'
'Nay, nay,' quod he, 'as ever mote I thryve!
It is a thing wel bet than swiche fyve.'

'Ye, holy god!' quod she, 'what thing is that?
What? bet than swiche fyve? ey, nay, y-wis!
For al this world ne can I reden what
It sholde been; som jape, I trowe, is this;
And but your-selven telle us what it is,
My wit is for to arede it al to lene;
As help me god, I noot nat what ye mene.'

'And I your borow, ne never shal, for me,
This thing be told to yow, as mote I thryve!'
'And why so, uncle myn? why so?' quod she.
'By god,' quod he, 'that wole I telle as blyve;
For prouder womman were ther noon on lyve,
And ye it wiste, in al the toun of Troye;
I jape nought, as ever have I joye!'

The verse, flawlessly metrical, weaves itself through
and around the light-hearted, gaily colloquial, irresponsible chatter, without an instant's check to its
sparkling flow. And the dialogue in the *Somnour's
Tale* between the Friar and the sick man Thomas
and Thomas's wife is unmatched for its revelation of
character, not only through the meanings which
words convey, but also through the very cast of the
suave, unctuous, hypocritical sentences. No one who
reads with ear as well as eye—and an ear no less than
an eye is a *sine qua non* for the reading of Chaucer—
can fail to catch the subtly characterized inflexions
of the Friar's voice. Read as Chaucer's contemporaries read it, there is no such body of flexible, musical
narrative verse as his in English—and none (at its
best) so superbly forthright and direct.

Finally, I am not greatly concerned about Chaucer's alleged defect of 'the σπουδαιότης, the high and

excellent seriousness, which Aristotle assigns as one of the grand virtues of poetry'. The poet who wrote the closing stanzas of the *Troilus*, and the Invocation to the Virgin in the Prologue of the Second Nun, and the Prioress's Prologue and Tale, and the noble balade *Truth*; whose memory was enriched from the wisdom of Boethius and the Bible; who was moved by the beauty of the hymns and the service of the Church, and who turned at will to the sublimest cantos of the *Purgatorio* and the *Paradiso*—that poet was not deficient in seriousness, high or deep. He had, to be sure, no 'message'. But his sanity ('He is', said Dryden, 'a perpetual fountain of good sense'), his soundness, his freedom from sentimentality, his balance of humorous detachment and directness of vision, and above all his large humanity—those are qualities which 'give us', to apply Arnold's own criterion, 'what we can rest upon'. And we should be hard put to it to name another poet with clearer title to rank with those who, in Philip Sidney's words, 'teach by a divine delightfulness'.

It is fairly obvious, I suppose, that I like Chaucer. I have made no effort to conceal the fact. And there is, after all, but one phrase in which to take leave of him. 'Here', said the sanest of all his admirers and critics—'Here is God's plenty.' And from the fragments only of that 'goddes foyson' I have gathered up six slender baskets full.

PRINTED IN GREAT BRITAIN
AT THE UNIVERSITY PRESS, OXFORD
BY VIVIAN RIDLER
PRINTER TO THE UNIVERSITY